Mealtime Habits
of the Messiah

Also by Conrad Gempf

Jesus Asked.

Mealtime Habits
of the Messiah

40 Encounters with Jesus

CONRAD GEMPF

ZONDERVAN™

GRAND RAPIDS, MICHIGAN 49530 USA

ZONDERVAN™

Mealtime Habits of the Messiah
Copyright © 2005 by Conrad Gempf

Requests for information should be addressed to:
Zondervan, *Grand Rapids, Michigan 49530*

Library of Congress Cataloging-in-Publication Data

Gempf, Conrad H.
    Mealtime habits of the Messiah : 40 encounters with Jesus / Conrad Gempf.—
1st ed.
      p. cm.
    Includes indexes.
    ISBN-10: 0-310-25717-4 (pbk.)
    ISBN-13: 978-0-310-25717-2
    1. Jesus Christ—Person and offices. I. Title.
BT203.G47 2005
232.9—dc22

                                       2005001446

Interior design by Beth Shagene

Printed in the United States of America

05 06 07 08 09 10 11 12 /❖ DCI/ 10 9 8 7 6 5 4 3 2 1

For Shanese
With bunches of love and gratitude

Table of Contents

Spiritual and Radical

Crucified and Resurrected

Conclusion

Foreword
by Rob Lacey

The book you're holding is playful and fun as well as scholarly and serious; the book you're holding is scholarly and serious. It's both a right brain *and* a left brain thing.

So often when we come to write about the most remarkable story in the world—the story of Jesus—the gravity of the situation drags us down. The world-changing nature of the material switches us into oh-so-earnest mode as we cave into the dominant voices in our heads: "But it's got to be intellectually definitive", or "It must show due reverence" or even "Something this important can't actually be enjoyable!"

Wrong!

Or maybe not "wrong", just "not fully right"! As a wise bishop once (well, more than once) said to me, "It's rarely 'either/or'; it's more often 'both/and'." Of course we need Intellectual Rigour, Respect, Serious Scholarship, but at what stage do these fine attributes morph into Academic Arrogance and Ivory Tower Isolation in a false-nose-and-glasses disguise? Maybe this is why the word *academic* has started to mean "irrelevant"—"Ah yes, but that's purely academic." What have we done?!

So, yes—pleeease—let's be intelligent in our handling of the life-changing story of Jesus, but intelligent in the fullest sense of that word. If we only pay attention to these voices clamouring for our attention, then we run the risk of drowning out another voice: that of the little boy standing at the door, scruffy clothes and dirt-caked knees, asking, "Can you come out to the park to play?" Don't blame me, but wasn't it Jesus who said the kingdom of Heaven belongs to such as these?

As an author, theatrical storyteller and performance poet, I'm well aware of the noise pollution in my own head, which effectively mutes the voice that speaks for what I know to be the most important element of creativity—the voice that speaks for Play. And Play is an elusive concept—even calling it a "concept" runs the risk of it evaporating from the heat of over-analysis. But if we don't ever just "kick the ball around", if we don't release ourselves from the handcuffs of well-meaning solemnity, then we're unlikely to have any creative "aha!" moments at all.

The home address of Play is way over in the right side of that most important organ of ours—the Metropolis of the Brain. Play hangs out on the bohemian side of town where the creative, pictorial and emotional activity happens, often after dark when most of the lights in the office blocks have been turned off. Sadly, few people travel between the two areas and Brain City is sometimes reminiscent of a Cold War–era Berlin with a wall blocking free access for those wishing to make the best of both worlds.

There are plenty of people writing about Jesus from the confines of the Left Brain Homeland of rational and systematic logical thought. But any study of Jesus will have to conclude that he himself was just as at home in the academic world as he was in the creative world. He was found debating with the Pharisees on the minutiae of Old Testament theology as well as constructing new parables that would stimulate the imagination of his audience and, therefore, resonate with their visual memories long after most had forgotten last week's synagogue sermon.

So should we bin all the left brain critiques of Jesus' mission? Nooo! Not either/or but both/and. We need to balance this wealth of writing with an increased awareness of Jesus' amazing creative spark: his gift for metaphor; his ability to conceal meaning as well as explain it; his skill at "portraying it" more than "saying it"; his "stage presence", holding an audience of thousands by just(!) telling stories; his "out of the box" thinking; his ability to adapt to new situations; his freedom from formulaic approaches; his belief in the power of a simple story to land and scatter into a thousand different applications according to the situation of each listener. Brilliant stuff!

In this book Conrad Gempf displays a similar ability: he has undoubted intellectual caliber, but he also has the freedom to allow this analytical ability to be "taken over the park", to kick around ideas on the poetic side of his brain.

His post–Berlin Wall brain makes many creative lateral thinking connections that he then brings back to the office to dissect and analyze.

The final product—this stimulating book—means his reader will always be making new discoveries with him. The mental commentary of the reader while digesting this book will be less along the lines of "Yes, I knew that" or "Well, that's something to add to my Jesus database of useful facts". It'll sound far more like, "Oh, I didn't think you were allowed to ask that!," "Well, if that's the case, then maybe I can play around with this idea" and even "That's funny—I'll remember that!"

Gempf's well balanced approach will, I'm sure, generate a desire to discuss further, to consider other possibilities. It will put fuel in the tanks of all our journeys toward wholeness and purpose. Good on him! Good on us! I just hope, with all this ability to catalyze discussion and intrigue, that Conrad Gempf hasn't made his personal email available to his readers—or his inbox will be so full that he'll never have any time to write another book for the rest of his life!

Rob Lacey, Cardiff, Wales
December 2004

Acknowledgments

I t's so obvious it probably doesn't need saying, but on the other hand, how can I leave it out? All our gratitude is due to God without whom the universe would never have gotten off the ground, much less the historical events described in this book, much less the book itself. Thanks be to God for his indescribable gifts.

I'm thankful to him, too, for wonderful family, colleagues and friends who made this book possible. My wife, Shanese, to whom this book is dedicated, and my children, Kat and Alistair, have been supportive, encouraging, sympathetic and full of love, and I'd be lost without them. My great friends Brett Jordan and Antony Billington have laughed at, argued with, scribbled over and, literally as well as figuratively, punched holes in early drafts of all this material. Glyn Norman also read the manuscript and helped me tighten the argument in several places, which was especially kind of him seeing how I've pretty much wiped out the book of encounters he wanted to write. There's a handful of other people who read or heard some bits of this and also tried to argue some sense into me. Not all will regard themselves as successful, I'm afraid, but I'm grateful for the input of Robin Sanderson, Rick Riggall, Meic Pearse and Graham McFarlane. It's likely that errors of brain and slips of fingers still remain in these pages, but these folks tried their best to fix me.

I'm also very grateful for the good ships Zondervan and London School of Theology; may God bless them and all who sail in them. A special conspiratorial "ahoy, there" to Derek, Anna, Robert, Steve, Tony, Steve, Stan, Amy, Elspeth, Angela, Lyn, Maryl and Curt.

Further afield, greetings to Chris, Len, Dwight, Steve, Tracy, Ron, Terry, Jon, Andy, David, Graham, Si, Anthony, Pete, Jason, James and Dale with thanks for the concrete encouragements in virtual environments.

Ethical and Aesthetic Environmental Impact Statement: No Microsoft products were used by the author in the composition of this book.

Introduction

Catering on Planet Earth

Jesus said to them, "Come and have breakfast."

John 21:1-14

Afterward Jesus appeared again to his disciples, by the Sea of Galilee. It happened this way: Simon Peter, Thomas (also known as Didymus), Nathanael from Cana in Galilee, the sons of Zebedee, and two other disciples were together. "I'm going out to fish," Simon Peter told them, and they said "We'll go with you." So they went out and got into the boat, but that night they caught nothing.

Early in the morning, Jesus stood on the shore, but the disciples did not realize that it was Jesus.

He called out to them, "Friends, haven't you any fish?"

"No," they answered.

He said, "Throw your net on the right side of the boat and you will find some." When they did, they were unable to haul the net in because of the large number of fish.

Then the disciple whom Jesus loved said to Peter, "It is the Lord!" As soon as Simon Peter heard him say, "It is the Lord," he wrapped his outer garment around him (for he had taken it off) and jumped into the water. The other disciples followed in the boat, towing the net full of fish, for they were not far from shore, about a hundred yards. When they landed, they saw a fire of burning coals there with fish on it, and some bread.

Jesus said to them, "Bring some of the fish you have just caught."

Simon Peter climbed aboard and dragged the net ashore. It was full of large fish, 153, but even with so many the net was not torn. Jesus said to them, "Come and have breakfast." None of the disciples dared ask him, "Who are you?" They knew it was the Lord. Jesus came, took the bread and gave it to them, and did the

17

same with the fish. This was now the third time Jesus appeared to the disciples after he was raised from the dead.

J esus was killed because of the way he ate." You'd be hard-pressed to find a cooler soundbite about the gospels than that statement by New Testament scholar Robert Karris. I so wish I'd thought of it first.

Compared to other biographies (except maybe those of famous gourmets and chefs) the gospels are bursting with meals and foods and daily bread. I'll be your tour guide through many stories about Jesus, whether they include grub or not. I've carved up the book into four main portions, corresponding to different facets of Jesus' life and work: (1) he was a teacher and more than a teacher; (2) he was a miracle worker and a healer; (3) he was a spiritual and radical guy; and (4) he was crucified and resurrected. It didn't surprise me to find meals playing a role in at least one or two of the encounters in all four sections.

But this story, Jesus cooking breakfast in John 21, baffles me. I don't know which of the four sections it belongs in. It's a resurrection appearance, of course, but there's also a miracle involved. Just under the surface, there's a lot of teaching about community and spirituality; so take your pick, really. But with such a great story, it's better to just drink it in than to take the time and energy to classify it. First stop, ladies and gentlemen, the Sea of Tiberias, aka the Sea of Galilee.

As the disciples return from an unproductive nightshift—*bam!*—there's Jesus. Only, as frequently occurs in the resurrection appearances, they don't realize it's Jesus. Whenever there's this lack of recognition, Jesus counters it not with words, as we would ("Hey, it's me!"), but with some unmistakable *action*. (I'll tell you about some of those other incidents later in the book.) With these fishermen, he reprises the net thing he did when some of the fishermen met him for the very first time (Luke 5:4–11). That does the trick. As if in replay of his first call, Peter leaves the boat and the nets and his friends behind, jumping straight into the water even though it wouldn't have taken long to land the boat. And he swims this time; getting to Jesus doesn't always involve walking on water.

When they get to shore, what do the disciples find? The risen Lord, master of time and space, who holds the galaxies in place and who knows all people's hearts and will be both the judge and the criterion on the last day.

And he's sitting there smoking 'em a few kippers for breakfast.

C'mon now, you've got to love him for that. If you read some of these so-called secret gospels, often written hundreds of years later by heretics who didn't really know Jesus, you'll find a risen Lord who is a glorious but ghostly oracle answering all their questions about the guardians of the seven heavens, the meaning of material reality and object-oriented programming languages. Not our Jesus. He's concentrating on turning over the pita bread to keep it from burning, just the way he concentrated on drawing in the sand in the "cast the first stone" story in John 8—unconcerned with the people around him, apparently. Yeah, right.

And then, just when we think he's going to look up and multiply his few fishes and loaves to feed all those disciples, we remember he's already multi-plied fishes: their nets are full.

What comes next is the most amazing and gracious thing, and the bit I love the best. Jesus is frying fish. He supplied a miraculous catch. What does he do and say next?

He makes just the right number of fish levitate out of the net and directly into the pan, right? No.

He says, "Have some of these fish already in my pan"? Wrong.

"Bring me some of the fish I've supplied for you"? Nope.

Here it is. He says, "Bring some of the fish you have just caught."

Excuse me? The fish *you* have caught? What did *they* have to do with it? By themselves they caught nothing. And it took them the whole night to do it.

Want to know what Jesus is really like? It doesn't get much better than this. He wants us to bring "our" fish, "our" talents, "our" service, "our" faith. Never mind that none of these are "ours" except as a gift. But he's serious. He's willing to regard them as ours; he wants our gifts, generously crediting us with generosity.

Have breakfast with Jesus: BYOF.

Most of the other stories I'll tell you about fall more neatly into one cate-gory or another. Take the first section, "Teacher and More". Arguably the cen-tral theme of Jesus' teaching was the kingdom of God. On a number of occasions he likened it to a huge dinner party with some surprises on the guest list. Also within the section on teaching we'll ask why Jesus didn't just say what he meant instead of beating around the bush with all these little stories and questions; we'll have a quick look at his most famous chunk of teaching; we'll investigate why he didn't have business cards with the name "Jesus Christ, Messiah, Second Person of Trinity" but used the ambiguous title "Son of Man"; and we'll spend some time thinking through the importance of teaching to Jesus himself and to the gospel writers. I'll even tell you just a little more than you wanted to know about the mysterious and secret document known only as Q. Shhh.

The miracle stories are probably the most fun, so this section is longer than the rest. We'll look at all manner of strange goings-on, including Jesus' somewhat tempestuous relationship with the Sea of Galilee. Back to our food and drink theme: there's the time Jesus lost some coins in the first century equivalent of a Coke machine and reduced it to a smoking heap of nuts and bolts, and the time he fed thousands of people on short notice with an inexperienced catering staff. There are also healings and exorcisms to examine, including a bunch of blind guys, ungrateful patients, a person who pops up from behind to siphon off some of Jesus' power, another who descends from above (through a hole in the roof), a guy whom Jesus healed of excessive body odor (though that was the least of his problems), and the time that Jesus could have quite properly said, "Go to hell", to a whole legion and didn't.

His radical spirituality involved Jesus in the main activity that Karris had in mind: having "table fellowship" with tax collectors and sinners. In those days, eating with people implied acceptance and a level of intimacy. In this section we'll also look at how Jesus prayed in public and in private, at his ultra-Jewish spirituality, and at his angry reactions and refusal to accept evil on the part of those who thought themselves holy.

Even more meals feature in the final section on Jesus' death and resurrection. There's the Last Supper, of course, but also the invitation to come in for a meal after the walk to Emmaus and a wonderful incident in which the risen Jesus materializes before the astonished disciples and asks, "Got anything to eat?" We'll also look at whether it would have been possible for Jesus to avoid the whole crucifixion business, how Pilate handled his tricky political situation, and how the people who loved Jesus had as hard a time adjusting to his being back as they did to his being gone.

We've included the Scripture passages at the start of each "encounter". We've also put some thought questions at the end of each. Even if you don't find those particular questions helpful, let their presence be a reminder to take time to ponder and even pray about what you've read and how you might respond. Throughout this book, you'll see and hear a very human Jesus who spoke about and did supernatural things unlike anyone else who ever lived, but also a divine Son of God who shows up on planet earth and waits and cooks and eats.

Make sure you show up too. Make it a real encounter.

Come and have breakfast.

Suggestions for Further Thought

On the matter of fish that Jesus provides but reckons as ours, a friend once pointed out that we find it easy to pray and ask for prayer when we're doing something unusual, outside our competence. But how often do we pray for the routine, the things that we think we've got under control? What fish are you taking for granted?

Is God interested in the "fish"—the nouns—at all? Or is he only interested in the verbs—the willingness to give and receive?

When on Earth, Do as the Earthlings Do

Have the same attitude of mind Christ Jesus had.

Philippians 2:1–18

Therefore if you have any encouragement from being united with Christ, if any comfort from his love, if any common sharing in the Spirit, if any tenderness and compassion, then make my joy complete by being like-minded, having the same love, being one in spirit and of one mind. Do nothing out of selfish ambition or vain conceit. Rather, in humility value others above yourselves, not looking to your own interests but each of you to the interests of the others.

In your relationships with one another, have the same attitude of mind Christ Jesus had:

> Who, being in very nature God,
> did not consider equality with God something to be used
> to his own advantage;
> rather, he made himself nothing,
> by taking the very nature of a servant,
> being made in human likeness.
> And being found in appearance as a human being,
> he humbled himself
> by becoming obedient to death –
> even death on a cross!

Therefore God exalted him to the highest place
and gave him the name that is above every name,
that at the name of Jesus every knee should bow,
in heaven and on earth and under the earth,
and every tongue acknowledge that Jesus Christ is Lord,
to the glory of God the Father.

Therefore, my dear friends, as you have always obeyed—not only in my presence, but now much more in my absence—continue to work out your salvation with fear and trembling, <u>for it is God who works in you to will and to act in order to fulfill his good purpose</u>.

Do everything without grumbling or arguing, so that you may become blameless and pure, "children of God without fault in a warped and crooked generation." Then you will shine among them like stars in the sky as you hold firmly to the word of life. And then I will be able to boast on the day of Christ that I did not run or labor in vain. But even if I am being poured out like a drink offering on the sacrifice and service coming from your faith, I am glad and rejoice with all of you. So you too should be glad and rejoice with me.

n the first of our introductory encounters, I presented the main sections into which this book is divided. To introduce three major themes that undergird the whole of the book, I've taken you to another New Testament passage. Most of the time we'll jump inside stories from the gospels, but here at the beginning and again at the end of the book, a few other passages are muscled in. This is the chief of them, a passage that has never left me alone. Even though it comes in a letter written by Paul, most of us in the New Testament business think there's a part of it he didn't write himself, a bit he quotes from an older Christian hymn both he and the Philippians know. It's easy to spot in most Bibles: verses 6 through 11 will usually have wider margins, typeset as poetry.

Through the use of this hymn, Paul is pleading with his readers to have the same attitude of mind as Christ (Phil. 2:5). But what does that mean? This is the first of the themes running through the book: <u>we're to imitate Christ</u>, but how? At times believers in the church actively sought their own deaths, preferably at the hands of enemies of the Gospel, to imitate Christ. Hey, if you're willing to ask yourself, "What would Jesus do?" at some point you've got to face the fact that he deliberately set his face toward death. There is a thin line between the humility of following in the Master's footsteps and the *chutzpah* of "Anything he can do, I can do." He is meant to be a model, but we also know that he is unique. We'll look at this in more detail later, but it blows out of the proverbial water any simple notion of mimicking Jesus. In each of the four facets of Jesus' life, we'll face this, the first of our three themes—the imitation of Christ.

New Testament specialists can't agree on how the original hymn behind Philippians 2:6–11 should be divided up and structured. But we all agree on how it should be graphed: down down down, up up up. Jesus comes down from a high place, all the way down to the humiliating death on a cross, then God raises him up to a place of high exaltation. Here comes the second thread woven through the book, and it follows from the first. Most of us probably have the notion that Jesus' mission on earth was unique. But what exactly was that unique mission? Was "down down down" the point or merely a necessary preliminary to "up up up"? In each section, we'll be considering this kind of thing. Did he come here primarily to teach? Did he come primarily to heal and do spiritual warfare with demons? Is the real meaning of the life of Jesus to be found in his radical spirituality, to model a spiritual way of living for us to emulate? Or finally, was his goal the cross? Or the resurrection? All those facets are important, but was any one of them the center?

The Philippians passage at least hints at the third theme you'll find coming up over and over again in the book: the trustworthiness of the gospels. This is something I deal with a lot in my day job. Lots of modern stuff about the New Testament assumes that it's all unreliable religious propaganda. And the attitude behind these kinds of views often leaks out into TV documentaries and lately even into fiction. The media fasten onto the weird and unlikely speculations. Oooh, maybe the gospel accounts are wrong and Jesus was actually married. Sure, the "evidence" is all from hundreds of years later than the gospels and comes from very dubious sources, but who wants to get into all that? Let the experts argue about nutrition while we gorge ourselves on what's tasty.

Okay, so I get a little emotional. Before we get too far in our journey together, I want to show you that you don't have to speculate about strange ideas in order for Jesus' life and teaching to be fascinating. But I'm also hoping you'll pick up how unlikely it is that the biblical accounts can be dismissed as merely the fictional "official spin" of the church. Traditionally, this comes up in its most pointed form in the accounts of the miracles, but the theme will surface in other contexts as well.

Philippians is characteristic of the biblical account in terms of its restraint. The picture painted by skeptics is of an official church hierarchy anxious to maintain control by force-feeding and hard-selling people a doctored authorized version of events. In contrast, Paul writes about a glorious and triumphant Christ, but only after being completely honest about Jesus' servanthood and humiliation on the cross. His conclusion is not that Christians and their leaders should regard themselves as the greatest, but that they too should be servants. Sometimes Paul is portrayed as some power-hungry autocrat, telling his underlings that God wants them to serve him (Paul) "without grumbling or arguing" (Phil. 2:14).

How far that is from the truth! Paul applies all this to himself as well. And he's not writing from a palace, urging the Philippians to send more goodies. No, he's writing from prison. He's not the Central Committee; he's the imprisoned dissident. I've read the research on first century prison conditions, and believe me, Paul knows all about humiliation and being a servant. Don't believe for a second that he left his promising and safe career in official Judaism for a cushy leadership position. He imitated Jesus, giving up everything safe in order to get that treasure buried in the field in Jesus' parable (Matt. 13:44–46).

More about Paul in another book. It's to Jesus' parables and questions we'll turn now.

Suggestions for Further Thought

The three major questions I want to explore in this book are (1) how do people rightly imitate Christ, (2) what was the core of Jesus' mission on earth, and (3) to what extent do the gospels contain "spin" by the early church to suit its needs? On some questions I'm probably more predictable than others. What would be your first stab answers to these questions?

How do you understand verses 6 and 7 of the Philippians passage? "Who, being in very nature God, did not consider equality with God something to be used to his own advantage; rather, he made himself nothing." What aspects of divine nature do you think he gave up, and what aspects did he keep?

Teacher and More

Parables and Questions

The master commended the dishonest manager because he had acted shrewdly.

Luke 16:1-9

Jesus told his disciples: "There was a rich man whose manager was accused of wasting his possessions. So he called him in and asked him, 'What is this I hear about you? Give an account of your management, because you cannot be manager any longer.'

"The manager said to himself, 'What shall I do now? My master is taking away my job. I'm not strong enough to dig, and I'm ashamed to beg—I know what I'll do so that, when I lose my job here, people will welcome me into their houses.'

"So he called in each one of his master's debtors. He asked the first, 'How much do you owe my master?'

"'Nine hundred gallons of olive oil,' he replied.

"The manager told him, 'Take your bill, sit down quickly, and make it four hundred and fifty.'

"Then he asked the second, 'And how much do you owe?'

"'A thousand bushels of wheat,' he replied.

"He told him, 'Take your bill and make it eight hundred.'

"The master commended the dishonest manager because he had acted shrewdly. For the people of this world are more shrewd in dealing with their own kind than are the people of the light. I tell you, use worldly wealth to gain friends for yourselves, so that when it is gone, you will be welcomed into eternal dwellings."

P eople who know nothing else about Jesus will still know they're expected to regard him as one of the greatest teachers who ever lived. It's not that they have some misconception that he went to Harvard or Cambridge. No one ever confuses Jesus with Hawking or Einstein or da Vinci. In fact, as far as we know, he never studied formally at all, not even to be a Galilean rabbi.

And his teaching didn't take the form of a monograph or a notebook full of primitive helicopters and spring-driven cars or even a chalkboard scrawled with formulae about the speed of light. His fame as a teacher seems totally out of proportion to his education and body of published work.

Instead, questions are typical of Jesus' teaching, and I'm not talking about the "Socratic method" either. Jesus doesn't prove to people that they know more than they think they know by asking them a series of deceptively easy questions. His questions are not usually about cold facts. Rather, he's interested in attitudes. He's not asking you to recall data but to make a judgement and a decision.

We've all heard that Jesus taught by telling stories—parables. In some ways, his parables do the same thing as his questions. Somehow, you get wrapped up in the course of the story so you're forming an opinion and choosing sides. And then almost without fail, the decision you make comes back to haunt you.

Ask someone what a parable is, and not many can refuse the temptation to tell you one, usually the prodigal son or the good Samaritan. The best-remembered, best-loved of Jesus' parables are the long, involved stories. But he also told much shorter ones and medium-length ones. In fact, as Mark 4:34 says, he was *always* talking in parables: "He did not say anything to them without using a parable." It's like it was a policy decision: no product packaging without a bar code, no teaching without a parable.

Mark goes on to say, however, that "when he was alone with his own disciples, he explained everything" (v. 34). Oh, ho! This clearly shows that the parables were not, as some believe, told in order to make difficult concepts easy to understand. Jesus had to *explain* them, even to his followers. If he knew how to explain them—how to make the teaching clearer than it was—why didn't he just lose the stories and start out with the explanations?

The answer is in one of Jesus' talks with his disciples about the sower and the soils story. There he explains the parables are appropriate because he's not in the persuading business but in the business of presenting opportunities. People might be talked into just about anything against their wills by someone really clever. Parables, in contrast, allow those willing to hear to do so but also allow the others to see but not see, hear but not understand (Matt. 13:11–19).

This parable I had you read about the dishonest manager bugs my students more than any other. I would have expected other passages to be more disturbing. For instance, in Luke 11:21–22 Jesus compares himself to a burglar, come to take what isn't his by stealth and force (see also Matt. 24:43–44, the thief in the night). Even worse, how about the time Jesus talks about prayers? If the average Christian was trying to explain why prayers sometimes appear to go unanswered, would she ever come up with a story like Luke 11:5–8, where the friend doesn't want to get up to supply bread, or Luke 18:2–8 about the widow and the sleeping judge? God is asleep in bed, and the first few times you ask, he's saying, "Go away"?! These are parables you'd think *should* bug London School of Theology students. These, however, they take in stride.

But the dishonest manager story is about something really sacred—money! Or maybe more important, Jesus seems to be advocating bribery and confusing friendship with a bought allegiance. And then, even worse, he's seeming to say buying people off is somehow connected with getting into heaven. It's verse 9 of that story that bewilders: "I tell you, use worldly wealth to gain friends for yourselves, so that when it is gone, you will be welcomed into eternal dwellings."

I suspect this statement is the real problem. It's not that my students are more jealous to guard the reputation of money than God. Rather, they instinctively sense the weaknesses and dangers of the capitalist system in which they live. I don't want to talk politics or economics here; my only point is that for someone in our culture to do what this manager is doing is a lot more insidious and spiritually dangerous than it would be in some other cultures. For us to have a "bad feeling" about this parable is probably a good sign.

There's no way Jesus is advocating bribery or bought relationships—you know that from his other teachings. And lest we mistake the message, the gospel writer emphasizes it by including some of that teaching later in the same chapter. "If you have not been trustworthy in handling worldly wealth, who will trust you with true riches?" (16:11)

Here's the thing: the "friend at midnight" parable is not about bread. The story of the shrewd manager isn't about money at all. Don't draw any conclusions about money from this; that's what the other bits of the chapter are telling you. The point is when you realize your present situation isn't going to last forever, you need to change the way you act. It's about acting on changed priorities—thinking about the future rather than about the present. At the start of the parable, the steward has been accused of wasting possessions. By the end of the parable, whatever else is going on, he's no longer careless with the possessions but using them to great effect. Here's a message for our "Whatever" mind-set, which preaches the importance of living in the now. Whoa! That's not Christianity. Jesus is all about intentionally using the present to influence the future.

Remember the parables about the man who discovers there's treasure in a field and the pearl merchant who finds the one perfect pearl (both in Matt. 13:44–46)? Both guys rearrange their priorities and sell everything they have to obtain what they know is better. That's the same rearranging and reorienting that the dishonest manager does here. Jesus could have done the John-the-Baptist thing and shouted, "Repent, for the kingdom of God is at hand!" But he loves to ask questions and tell stories. He seems to commend dishonesty and wants you to think, *That can't be right, can it?* It's in the wrestling with the conundrum that you come to really feel his point. Like Jacob with the angel back in Genesis 32, only by wrestling with it are you likely to come out with a changed attitude.

I love Eugene Peterson's take on verse 8 in his paraphrase *The Message*: "Streetwise people are smarter in this regard than law-abiding citizens. They are on constant alert, looking for angles, surviving by their wits. I want you to be smart in the same way—but for what is *right*."

Suggestions for Further Thought

Is there some talent or possession you are squandering rather than using with intentionality? How are you going to fix it?

The word *streetwise* in this context makes me smile when I think of the Bible's description of heaven—the very streets made out of gold. To be streetwise in a way suitable for the City of God—what would that kind of savvy look like?

Sermon on the Mount

Be perfect, therefore, as your heavenly Father is perfect.

Matthew 5:43–48

"You have heard that it was said, 'Love your neighbor and hate your enemy.' But I tell you, love your enemies and pray for those who persecute you, that you may be children of your Father in heaven. He causes his sun to rise on the evil and the good, and sends rain on the righteous and the unrighteous. If you love those who love you, what reward will you get? Are not even the tax collectors doing that? And if you greet only your own people, what are you doing more than others? Do not even pagans do that? Be perfect, therefore, as your heavenly Father is perfect."

I must be nuts. With so much good stuff in the Sermon on the Mount running for the best part of three chapters in Matthew's gospel, I choose this bit to write about? Be perfect?! Any author in his or her right mind would pick something a bit more useful and practical and relevant.

Growing up evangelical in a well-enough-to-do suburb of the largest city in the wealthiest country in the world, when we talked about the Sermon on the Mount, we focused on more useful tidbits. The Beatitudes in Matthew 5, for instance. They're short and reassuring: "Blessed are the meek, for they will inherit the earth. Blessed are those who hunger and thirst for righteousness, for they will be filled" and like that. Now we're talking. And we loved the bit about the birds and the lilies of the field who don't have to worry about a thing. We want to inherit the earth, we want to be filled, we want to not have to worry about a thing.

Wake up, gang. We are not the meek. We rarely know what it means to hunger and thirst. When Jesus talked about worrying about food and worrying about clothes, he didn't mean getting serious about carbs or getting the look just right for the occasion. There are people in the world who need to hear the promises and reassurances of Jesus, but chances are, if you've got the resources to be reading this book, you're not among them.

I've learned a lot of stuff about the Bible in general and Jesus' teaching in particular. One of the most important things is very simple but very neglected: you shouldn't focus on those passages in the Bible that contain answers you resonate with. Instead, focus on passages that address situations that resonate with your situation. So it's not, "Are there any biblical characters who received the kind of message I want to hear?" but rather, "What does the Bible say to characters who are in a similar situation to my own?"

For instance, too many rich people name and claim promises like "God will provide". Instead, maybe we should make little religious knick-knack vases with dried flowers in them and "Woe to the rich" embossed in gold letters. Yes, Jesus loves us all dearly, but we're told he disciplines those whom he loves (Prov. 3:12; Heb. 12:6). Where are the t-shirts with the motto "Jesus had stern words for people like me"?

Be perfect as your heavenly Father is perfect. This isn't just a blip in the sermon. Earlier in the chapter is another passage we love to ignore—the one referring to the Pharisees and teachers of the law. We usually think their problem was taking the requirements of the Old Testament law too seriously. We cherish those passages where Jesus tells them to loosen up. Why? Not because we are in the same situation as the Pharisees, so we need to hear what Jesus told them. We love it because "Lighten up" is already our motto.

We're less happy to read about what Jesus taught his disciples who weren't as gung-ho on the Law: "Do not think that I have come to abolish the Law . . . Not the smallest letter, not the least stroke of a pen, will by any means disappear from the Law . . . Anyone who sets aside one of the least of these commands and teaches others accordingly will be called least in the kingdom of heaven . . . Unless your righteousness surpasses that of the Pharisees and the teachers of the law, you will certainly not enter the kingdom of heaven" (Matt. 5:17–20).

Jesus' Sermon on the Mount is not easy or comforting. It's difficult and offensive. At times, it reads like an argument in favor of the Thought Police. Twenty-first century people, even Christians, will have a hard time getting their heads round a morality that says looking at a member of the opposite sex and thinking certain ways is as bad as adultery, or that disliking someone enough to call them a fool is risking being sent to hell (Matt. 5:21–28). What is going on here? What happened to that nice Jesus who doodles in the sand and saves an adulteress from stoning? Again, situations, folks. Is it surprising that he has a very different message for prostitutes than he does for closet Peeping Toms? And which of those messages is meant for us, do you suppose?

Camels and needles, is it really impossible for the "haves" like us to enter the kingdom? No, even the impossible is possible with God—through Jesus. But we need to remember he provides the only way for nice, reasonable, freedom-loving people to get in. Aren't even godless pagans, tax collectors and politicians able to act nice and reasonable and freedom-loving? Big deal, says God.

Is this sermon a counsel of despair then? Is its primary objective to make us realize how great God's demands are and how impossible it is for us to meet them by our own strength? Is the purpose to cause us to rely on Jesus?

That is an important function that the sermon can serve. But wait, don't fade out from the specifics of its teachings and cut directly to the PowerPoint slide of the "Amazing Grace" remix too quickly. We cannot be like this, but we must be like this. Or rather, we must be becoming like this. Careful, it's not a new law. Throughout, Jesus says clearly that this is not about *external* observance of some regulations. Rather, it's about *inwardly* conforming to the character to which the laws have always pointed. It's not about being a law-abiding person; it's about being a good person in the sense that what's inside you is good. And your insides are going to be pretty grotty unless God, not you, is in complete charge in there.

So we must be becoming more and more like the Sermon on the Mount, and that means we can use the text as a test of ourselves—almost more as a test of our attitudes and mind-set than as a test of our outward actions. I believe that the Christian should read the sermon listening for alarm bells. Whatever culture you belong to, some parts of the sermon will sound right and others wrong. There'll be some aspects of it about which you'll say, "Yesss."

Stop celebrating and move on, because there will be others where you'll hear alarm bells. You'll want to rebel and say, "That can't be right!" Those are the parts of your spiritual life that you want to pray about and work on. Make that into the t-shirt. And wear it inside out.

Suggestions for Further Thought

Instead of focusing on the promises of the Bible, spend a little time looking for and thinking through the challenges. Do any immediately come to mind as relevant to you?

Does God really hold us responsible for our thought life as well as our actions? So is it sinful even to be tempted?

Who Do You Say I Am?

"But what about you?" he asked.

Matthew 16:13-23

When Jesus came to the region of Caesarea Philippi, he asked his disciples, "Who do people say the Son of Man is?"

They replied, "Some say John the Baptist; others say Elijah; and still others, Jeremiah or one of the prophets."

"But what about you?" he asked. "Who do you say I am?"

Simon Peter answered, "You are the Messiah, the Son of the living God."

Jesus replied, "Blessed are you, Simon son of Jonah, for this was not revealed to you by flesh and blood, but by my Father in heaven. And I tell you that you are Peter, and on this rock I will build my church, and the gates of death will not overcome it. I will give you the keys of the kingdom of heaven; whatever you bind on earth will be bound in heaven, and whatever you loose on earth will be loosed in heaven." Then he ordered his disciples not to tell anyone that he was the Messiah.

From that time on Jesus began to explain to his disciples that he must go to Jerusalem and suffer many things at the hands of the elders, the chief priests and the teachers of the law, and that he must be killed and on the third day be raised to life.

Peter took him aside and began to rebuke him. "Never, Lord!" he said. "This shall never happen to you!"

Jesus turned and said to Peter, "Get behind me, Satan! You are a stumbling block to me; you do not have in mind the concerns of God, but merely human concerns."

hen it comes to Jesus, the first thing you've got to realize is that "Christ" isn't his last name. People legitimately wondered whether Jesus was the Christ, and, of course, they couldn't tell by looking at his driver's license. Rather, it was a title: the Greek equivalent of the Hebrew messiah. Thus, when Peter comes to understand that Jesus is the Messiah, it's a big deal. It's apparently an even bigger deal than thinking he was one of the prophets sent by God. That's what the people say he is, and the story seems to demand that Peter's pronouncement be an advance on that opening bid. Messiah seems to be the right answer.

But what is a messiah? The word in Hebrew or Greek simply means "anointed". So that's it? Someone with a wet head? This is easy: grab some water balloons and let's congratulate us some messiahs! No, of course not. Anointing is a ceremony that means someone is chosen by God for a particular role or task. It's a word like *nominee* or *appointee*.

A prophet is a person chosen to bring God's message, often to a king or government that had lost its way in Israel. But a messiah is anointed to go beyond speaking about a situation to doing something about it. A messiah is more a doer than a teacher.

So if Jesus wants them to know that he's the Messiah, why doesn't he just tell them? All this teaching—five major sermons in Matthew—and so little of it is about who or what Jesus is. And even when the disciples figure it out, Jesus doesn't want them to use the title openly (Matt. 16:20). Why? Probably for two reasons, both related to the Messiah's task being seen in political or military terms. One was that Jesus didn't want to be arrested before "his hour", and the second was that he wanted to show his disciples how he wanted them to understand the title.

Jesus accepts Peter's use of the word *messiah*, but he prefers to teach about himself with the even odder title "Son of Man." You see it here in Jesus' question from Matthew 16:13: "Who do people say the Son of Man is?" Jesus uses it of himself in his humility: "Foxes have holes and birds have nests, but the Son of Man has no place to lay his head" (Matt. 8:20) and his coming humiliation: "The Son of Man is going to be delivered over to human hands" (Matt. 17:22 NIV). But it's also found in some triumphant cosmic passages like Matthew

25:31: "When the Son of Man comes in his glory, and all the angels with him, he will sit on his glorious throne."

This is a less well-known title, even though the phrase receives more Old Testament airtime than the term *messiah*. You'll see it all over the book of Ezekiel, starting with 2:1: "He said to me, 'Son of man, stand up on your feet and I will speak to you'" (NIV; see also 2:3, 6, 8; 3:1, 3, 4, 10, 17, 25 and many others). The use is similar to that in the well-known verse from the Psalms: "What is man that you care for him, the son of man that you think of him?" (8:4). It seems to mean "an ordinary guy".

The most famous passage in Jesus' day and ours, though, is undoubtedly Daniel 7, in which Daniel had visions of four freaky beasts followed by a contrasting fifth: "In my vision at night I looked, and there before me was one like a son of man, coming with the clouds of heaven. He approached the Ancient of Days and was led into his presence. He was given authority, glory and sovereign power; all peoples, nations and men of every language worshiped him. His dominion is an everlasting dominion that will not pass away, and his kingdom is one that will never be destroyed" (Dan. 7:13–14 NIV). Passages like Matthew 24:30 have this Son of Man in mind: "At that time the sign of the Son of Man will appear in the sky, and all the peoples of the earth will mourn. They will see the Son of Man coming on the clouds of heaven, with power and great glory."

His original hearers would not have had the luxury of a book full of sayings to cross-check. Each time Jesus used the phrase, his hearers would have had to think. Was he referring to himself or someone else? When he did refer to himself, did he mean just an ordinary guy, or did he mean the cloud rider who was like an ordinary guy? Who is he saying that he is?

Here's the nub: the very phrase Jesus uses to describe himself is just like his parables and questions—it sucks you in and forces you to make a decision about who he's most likely to be. He asks, "Who do you say that I am?" in many different ways.

But while Jesus avoided claiming the title of Messiah, much less God, in words, he made the claim in other ways. John's gospel is full of cryptic but direct comments about his identity. He is the bread of life and the living water and so on. One of the weirdest is in John 8:58: "Very truly I tell you . . . before Abraham was born, I am!" Something truly cosmic is going on there!

We'll see later how in all the gospels he claims a closer relationship with God than his opponents will have found comfortable. Perhaps most significantly for his original hearers, though, he claims to be involved in doing things that only God should be doing. Nowadays people won't believe something is a duck without checking its genetic material. In those days, what it was made out of was less important than whether it walked like a duck, swam like a duck and quacked like a duck. Jesus never claims he was involved in creation, though other New Testament books do say so. But he does claim to have an authority over sins that only God should have (Luke 5:21), he comes close to redrafting the Law given by God (see the repeated "But *I* tell you's" in Matt. 5:31–48), he says he'll be involved in the future judgement when he will be both the judge (John 5:26–30) and the criterion on which people will be judged (John 3:18).

Again, more about this later, but the peculiar thing is how much Jesus does claim about himself in an understated sort of way. You can never find that one great verse to pin down the Jehovah's Witnesses when they come calling, but if you read any gospel for more than a chapter or so, you'll come round to realize that Jesus gave himself, as the Son of Man, the starring role in all of reality. I keep waiting for the gospel in which some wise guy Pharisee says, "Oh, right, Jesus. What? Is *everything* about you?" And Jesus would just calmly stare him down and say, "What do *you* think?"

Suggestions for Further Thought

Being a messiah means being the answer to the big question. But Jesus wasn't primarily answering the main question people in his culture had, at least not in the way they expected. What are the big questions in our culture? How does Jesus answer and not answer them?

Who do you think Jesus is? What are the implications of that for you?

The Messianic Dinner Party

Blessed are those who will eat at the feast in the kingdom of God.

Luke 14:15-24

When one of those at the table with him heard this, he said to Jesus, "Blessed are those who will eat at the feast in the kingdom of God."

Jesus replied: "A certain man was preparing a great banquet and invited many guests. At the time of the banquet he sent his servant to tell those who had been invited, 'Come, for everything is now ready.'

"But they all alike began to make excuses. The first said, 'I have just bought a field, and I must go and see it. Please excuse me.'

"Another said, 'I have just bought five yoke of oxen, and I'm on my way to try them out. Please excuse me.'

"Still another said, 'I just got married, so I can't come.'

"The servant came back and reported this to his master. Then the owner of the house became angry and ordered his servant, 'Go out quickly into the streets and alleys of the town and bring in the poor, the crippled, the blind and the lame.'

"'Sir,' the servant said, 'what you ordered has been done, but there is still room.'

"Then the master told his servant, 'Go out to the roads and country lanes and compel them to come in, so that my house will be full. I tell you, not one of those who were invited will get a taste of my banquet.'"

Some cultures know how to throw a party; I'm not sure that we in the West really do. In first century Israel, an ordinary wedding banquet was something to look forward to. It was a community affair and it lasted for days. Imagine something of a cross between our wedding celebrations, Christmas and a week's vacation and you start to get the picture.

And the meals back then were one of the biggest things. In our age of microwavable packaged meals and lemon-fresh automatic dishwashers, most of us will have to concentrate to imagine what a chore the business of food preparation and cleaning up afterwards was for most human beings in the history of the planet.

We have a hard time grasping the value of fasting, for instance, because in our heads it's only about eating or not eating. But in the first century, the idea of fasting included the idea of freeing up time for prayer. In our culture, prayer-time has gone the way of food preparation: four minutes on the highest setting, stirring once halfway through the cycle; and then the whole mess stacked away, out of sight, set on automatic-normal. But in the first century, not needing meals during the day would free up a lot of time.

A banquet is almost like fasting but better—the guests receive special and extravagant party foods, but they're still freed up from all the preparation and cleaning-up duties—devoting that time instead to enjoying themselves with the rest of the guests. This is what Jesus says the kingdom of God is like: eating dinner out, a party.

But there's a wrinkle in our passage: the people on the guest list refuse the hospitality. The first two guests are easy to despise. They have new possessions, but it's pretty clear who possesses whom. Our culture knows this syndrome full well. To be fair, even though we fall into its snare often, we generally recognize when our computer is starting to run our lives for its own benefit. We catch ourselves spending time and energy downloading and installing this week's pile of security patches (which don't help us work any better; they're purely for the machine's benefit); or when we stop going to a shop we like because it's easier to park near a different shop we don't like as well—it's simpler to give in to the car's preferences.

For most of us Westerners, the third guy in Jesus' story is harder to blame. Our Western culture seems normal to us, but it's actually extremely unusual in the extent to which we focus on the individual rather than larger family or tribe or other community groupings. One of the unrecognized consequences of our emphasis on the individual is how it affects our definition of selfishness. Because we don't usually consider anyone other than ourselves, whatever we do for our spouse or our kids or our parents is seen as unselfish and altruistic. I am called by this parable to think not only beyond "me me me" but also beyond "me and mine".

If this is true for us of the family and close ties and cliques, the sharpest edge comes for the original audience in terms of thinking beyond their tribe and nation. A similar saying about the Messianic Dinner Party expands or clarifies the reversal theme: "There will be weeping . . . when you see Abraham, Isaac and Jacob and all the prophets in the kingdom of God, but you yourselves thrown out. People will come from east and west and north and south, and will take their places at the feast in the kingdom of God" (Luke 13:28–29).

The phrase "kingdom of God" dominates Jesus' teaching, and Christians have dithered about what it means. Once upon a time, people imagined that "kingdom" demanded you to think of a territory or place, as if God favored one geographic area or nation over another. "God bless our nation" is one thing; "God is on *our* side" is quite another. In reaction against that, the phrase "kingdom of God" fell out of fashion in the twentieth century. Christians began taking "kingdom" language to refer more to the *king* than the *-dom*. So now, it's more popular to talk about the king*ship* of God. Contemporary Christian songs and books are full of this kind of stuff: "Our God Reigns."

This, however, was more of an overreaction against a wrong view than a careful understanding of what the New Testament says. You don't have to read it very long before bumping into passages that are difficult to understand on this model. If kingdom means God's authority to rule, then it would be very strange for Jesus to say of little children "the reign of God belongs to such as these" (Luke 18:16, paraphrased). There are also all those passages about the kingdom being something you enter or out of which you can be thrown.

It's right not to see the kingdom of God as a physical country with boundaries, but it probably means something like a people or a community. It's a set of relationships or state of affairs in which God is recognized as King and Master and others are recognized as fellow subjects of the King. That's why the book of Revelation can say that through his blood, Jesus "has made us to be a kingdom and priests to serve his God and Father" (Rev. 1:6; see also 5:10). He's made us into the kingly authority of God? No. He's made us into a network of interrelated subjects of the one King.

The passage we've been looking at could refer to either "kingship" or "community". When Matthew introduces the parable (Matt. 22), we might interpret it as having the king's relationship with individuals in mind. Using his favorite alternate wording "kingdom of heaven", Matthew writes, "The kingdom of heaven is like a king who . . ." On the other hand, obviously, the whole image of a banquet with lots of guests is suggestive of the kingdom of God meaning kingdom in this sense of community.

The modern view of kingdom as kingship renders Christianity as basically an individual matter with community implications. But if kingdom really means kingdom, then community is integral, rather than a tacked-on implication. This explains why the phrase became such a catch-all for Jesus' ministry, concerned as it was with people as well as interior attitude toward God. Learning to live in the kingdom of God means living with our primary allegiance to the King and to each other rather than ourselves, our possessions or simply our immediate family. We can start now, even though the kingdom will exist in a new and final way in paradise, the wedding feast of the Lamb (Rev. 19:9). As Tony Campolo is fond of saying, the kingdom of God is a party!

Suggestions for Further Thought

Is the parable of the great banquet about judgement or about inclusion? Does Jesus really want us to think of God as someone who accepts the outcasts only when the "beautiful people" don't turn up?

For many Christians, the phrase "kingdom of God" is exclusively about the future. What elements of it should be present realities?

Come to Preach?

He has anointed me to proclaim good news to the poor.

Luke 4:16–30

He went to Nazareth, where he had been brought up, and on the Sabbath day he went into the synagogue, as was his custom. He stood up to read, and the scroll of the prophet Isaiah was handed to him. Unrolling it, he found the place where it is written:

> "The Spirit of the Lord is on me,
> because he has anointed me
> to proclaim good news to the poor.
> He has sent me to proclaim freedom for the prisoners
> and recovery of sight for the blind,
> to set the oppressed free,
> to proclaim the year of the Lord's favor."

Then he rolled up the scroll, gave it back to the attendant and sat down. The eyes of everyone in the synagogue were fastened on him. He began by saying to them, "Today this scripture is fulfilled in your hearing."

All spoke well of him and were amazed at the gracious words that came from his lips. "Isn't this Joseph's son?" they asked.

Jesus said to them, "Surely you will quote this proverb to me: 'Physician, heal yourself!' And you will tell me, 'Do here in your hometown what we have heard that you did in Capernaum.'"

"Truly I tell you," he continued, "prophets are not accepted in their hometowns. I assure you that there were many widows in Israel in Elijah's time, when the sky was shut for three and a half years and there was a severe famine throughout the land. Yet Elijah was not sent to any of them, but to a widow in Zarephath in the region of Sidon. And there were many in Israel with leprosy in the time of Elisha the prophet, yet not one of them was cleansed—only Naaman the Syrian."

All the people in the synagogue were furious when they heard this. They got up, drove him out of the town, and took him to the brow of the hill on which the town was built, in order to throw him off the cliff. But he walked right through the crowd and went on his way.

He's supposed to be the greatest teacher who ever lived, and look at the response of the audience in this story! Jesus said to proclaim or preach was part of his mission, but it didn't always go all that well, apparently. Here he beats a hasty and quasi-miraculous retreat. We'll have cause to mention his curious escape from the crowd again later, but now I want to focus on Jesus' statement of mission and what makes the crowd lose their cool.

The way Luke tells the story, it is Jesus' preaching that riles them. Before he opens his mouth, the people are full of praise for him (Luke 4:15). What turns them? Is it that this mere carpenter's son makes extravagant claims for himself? No, even after Jesus says that this Old Testament prophecy applies to him, the audience still seem to be on his side (4:21–22). How does he manage to provoke them to such open hostility by verse 28?

Let's look at those Old Testament claims first. Lukan scholars often call this passage Jesus' Inaugural Address, because the gospel writer, like a film editor, deliberately cuts to this scene after Jesus' baptism and temptation, even though he clearly knows Jesus did some noteworthy things elsewhere first. And it does seem to be setting out a mission statement or even a political manifesto. "If elected, I promise massive economic recovery (good news for the poor), freedom for all prisoners (of the Roman system), the elimination of eye disease, and may God bless America!" (4:18–19, paraphrased ever so slightly). Indeed, that's what his audience was probably hoping to hear, and they become excited when he seems to be giving them what they want. He is one of them, he has worked miracles elsewhere, now he will work miracles here where he belongs—time to strike up the band and release the balloons for the local boy made good and come home to do the business!

But, of course, the crowd is not on the same wavelength as Jesus. Look closely and you'll see he's holding a pin for those celebratory balloons. He explains the "Physician, heal yourself" thing in verse 23 this way: You guys expect me to do miracles for me and mine, but what if I told you the miracles are for foreigners? In reply to the hometown crowd's focus on their own felt needs, Jesus compared his own ministry not with that of Moses who helped free his own people at the exodus, nor with Joshua leading his own people into the land at the conquest, much less with Ezra or Nehemiah leading their own people back at the end of the exile/return to the land. Instead, he compares himself with prophets who functioned at a time more like the first century— a time when "Jewish" kings like Herod with foreign pagan influence ruled the land—the time of Elijah and Elisha. And despite the needs in Israel at the time, they saved their really cool stuff for outsider Gentiles and not for their own people.

This good news Jesus will be preaching in his mission has nothing to do with political or economic relief packages. He will heal a handful of people who are literally blind, as we'll see shortly, but mainly he'll be addressing another kind of blindness—spiritual blindness. Similarly, the prisons and other oppressions from which he promises release are not the obvious physical ones. John the Baptist is going to have a huge personal problem with this. John is sure about Jesus at first, but then sends his disciples to ask, "Are you the one . . . or should we expect someone else?" (Luke 7:20) Perhaps he asks precisely because Jesus said his mission was to release prisoners—meanwhile, good old J the B is waiting behind bars.

Jesus has come to preach, but it's a different kind of good news than anyone expected. It is both disappointing and amazing. Sometimes we Christians think the Jewish people were too limited when they looked for a military/political messiah rather than the spiritual one they got. But people in those days would have seen it the other way round. Anyone who thought their God was the kind of God who would bring the slaves in Egypt a mere "personal peace and freedom" while leaving them there making bricks would have been thinking of a too-limited God. Their God is the kind of force that bashes the walls of Jericho to smithereens and all you have to do is parade and blow the noise-makers in just the right way. Jesus' brand of messiahship looked to many to be selling God short and certainly selling his chosen nation, Israel, short. But again on the topic of his mission here, the snub is deliberate: "I have not come to call the righteous, but sinners" (Matt. 9:13).

Is good news all he has come to bring? Good preaching and teaching are nice . . . but is that it? Is it merely the promise of freeing captives, or is there a reality attached, even if not the one you would have expected? Jesus was a teacher, but that wasn't the center of his mission. There are passages in which Jesus is a bit more forthcoming about his purpose and goal. "I have come that they may have life, and have it to the full" (John 10:10), and "I have come into the world as a light, so that no one who believes in me should stay in darkness" (12:46). But contemplating his crucifixion and struggles in Gethsemane, he says, "Now my soul is troubled, and what shall I say? 'Father, save me from this hour'? No, it was for this very reason I came to this hour" (12:27).

And passages like this are not only in John's gospel. "The Son of Man did not come to be served, but to serve, and to give his life as a ransom for many" (Matt. 20:28). He didn't accomplish that by talking.

Suggestions for Further Thought

Go back to that Nazareth sermon and the description of Jesus' role there: good news to the poor and so on. Are those things meant to be literal or symbolic? Are they things he fulfilled in his lifetime, or are they future promises?

What do you think Jesus meant by "his hour" and his mission statements? What do you guess was his objective on earth?

Why St. Mark Would Have Hated Red-letter Bibles

He taught them as one who had authority.

Mark 1:21-28

They went to Capernaum, and when the Sabbath came, Jesus went into the synagogue and began to teach. The people were amazed at his teaching, because he taught them as one who had authority, not as the teachers of the law. Just then a man in their synagogue who was possessed by an evil spirit cried out, "What do you want with us, Jesus of Nazareth? Have you come to destroy us? I know who you are—the Holy One of God!"

"Be quiet!" said Jesus sternly. "Come out of him!" The evil spirit shook the man violently and came out of him with a shriek.

The people were all so amazed that they asked each other, "What is this? A new teaching—and with authority! He even gives orders to evil spirits and they obey him." News about him spread quickly over the whole region of Galilee.

You know what a red-letter Bible is, right? They're not as common as they used to be, but you still do find them around. They're like any other Bible, come in just about any translation, but in these, the four gospels are in Technicolor. Direct quotations of the Lord Jesus are printed with red ink to make them stand out. If you described such a volume to Mark, the author of the earliest of our gospels, he might have phoned his publisher to contractually forbid such a thing.

To explain why I think this, we have to look at the Scriptures in a way you may not be used to—I want to explain to you what we might call the *texture* of Scripture as well as the content. All the while that I was growing up and going to Bible studies, I knew something was missing . . . and now I'm sure this was it. We were studying the content of passages, and that's the right thing to study for the most part. That's what we're doing in most of the segments of this book. But I'll also be hinting at the texture. And in this segment at least, we'll be encountering the portrait of Jesus as much or more than encountering Jesus through the portrait.

Painting is a good analogy, actually. For most of us ordinary folks, the most important thing about a painting is the content. But if you look closely at Van Gogh's *Sunflowers* for instance, there's something about the way he's used a surprising color scheme, made little crosses in the background and heaped the paint onto the petals. You don't need to notice all of that to enjoy a painting, and everyone except a specialist knows that paying too much attention to that kind of stuff can actually spoil the appreciation of art—you probably know someone who can't sit still and enjoy a film because they're too busy talking about how the director did this or that special effect. But some awareness of texture can enhance your understanding of film or paintings or Scripture.

A prime example is the absurdity of having four gospels. Most evangelicals have thought a lot about what's in the gospels, but hardly ever about the fact that there are four. Imagine unpacking your new DVD player. You spend 15 minutes trying to grab the outside of the box with your knees and feet so you can actually get the Styrofoam padding to slide out of the box. Finally, out pop not only the player but four instruction manuals. Each contains a page or a diagram that none of the others do. There are large areas of overlap, but sometimes they'll recommend steps in a different sequence or have other variations.

There was a guy named Tatian early in the church's history who decided to do something about this public relations disaster before it was too late. He took the four gospels, a big scrapbook and some scissors and glue and sent out for pizza. By the end of the day, he had a floor full of narrow strips of paper and a scrapbook that contained every single story the gospels told about Jesus (but only one copy of each story—the fullest one) in chronological order. He had, in other words, a single gospel that left absolutely no content out of the original four. A lot of Christians would have preferred that to what we've got. If content were all that the fourfold gospels were about, there'd be no reason not to prefer it. But texture, friends, texture. Part of the very fabric and character of the gospels is that we have the several separate and individual accounts. There's relationship and texture there, not just content.

But here's something surprising. There's at least one gospel that was around at the time of these four that the church didn't keep. At least we don't have it anymore. It may or may not have once had a famous name attached to it; we don't know. Today we know it by a single letter, Q. This source and Mark were the earliest. Something like 98 percent of the contents of Mark can be found repeated in the longer gospels of Matthew and Luke. And just as they both used Mark, so they both used this Q. I have good reasons for thinking this, but I promise you don't want me to go into them here. Otherwise, before you know it, I'll be teaching you words like *synoptics* and *source criticism,* and pretty soon you won't have any friends left at all.

We have a pretty good idea of what Q looked like. It was almost exclusively about the things Jesus taught, what he said. That's a very natural book for disciples to write about their rabbi: a collection of his inspirational teachings—Quotations of Jesus.

How unlike Mark and the others, though. In fact, Mark in particular leans almost exactly the opposite direction. In our passage from Mark 1, the author tells us that Jesus was a teacher, but when it comes right down to it, Mark doesn't give his readers all that much of the content of what Jesus taught. Here's another related imbalance. Most people guess that Jesus lived about thirty-three years. Mark has sixteen chapters, so you'd think that'd work out to two years in each chapter. Well, all right, Mark chooses to focus on the three years of Jesus' public life, fair enough. Still, then you'd expect roughly one year to equal five chapters. Well, Mark takes his final five chapters to cover not one year but one week: the week of Jesus' trial, crucifixion and resurrection. It's clear this is the focus as well as the climax of Mark's work. And I think he's done it on purpose. It can only be speculation, but it seems likely that the earliest Christians would have come to prefer a gospel like Mark to a collection like Q. For Paul as well as for Mark, the most important thing about Christ was not what he said but that he came and that he died for us. To focus on the words of the great rabbi would be understandable, but would also be, ultimately, incomplete and inadequate.

Now (at last) you can see why I say that Mark the gospel writer would have been against red-letter Bibles. I think Paul would have been as well. Anything that makes it look as though the really important part of Jesus' life was the spiritual words he said is a misrepresentation of who he was. If Mark himself were to have put anything in a special type or color, it would have been his account of Easter week.

What Jesus did was more important than what he taught. But, of course, the teaching was also important when seen in its proper context. And that's why Luke and Matthew were successful in their attempts to take the teachings of Jesus out of Q and place them in an overall story that included his death and resurrection. They may well have been happier than Mark with Q and even with red-letter Bibles.

Suggestions for Further Thought

None of the epistles, not even Peter or John, quotes Jesus' teachings very much. We know they think his teaching has some importance; why is it absent then?

If the Q mind-set had won—if we thought that what he taught was more important than what he did—would we wear little golden scrolls around our necks instead of crosses? How else would Christianity be different?

Miracle Worker
and Healer

Full of Miracles?

News about him spread all over.

Matthew 4:23–25; 15:29–31

Jesus went throughout Galilee, teaching in their synagogues, proclaiming the good news of the kingdom, and healing every disease and sickness among the people. News about him spread all over Syria, and people brought to him all who were ill with various diseases, those suffering severe pain, the demon-possessed, those having seizures, and the paralyzed; and he healed them. Large crowds from Galilee, the Decapolis, Jerusalem, Judea and the region across the Jordan followed him.

Jesus left there and went along the Sea of Galilee. Then he went up on a mountainside and sat down. Great crowds came to him, bringing the lame, the blind, the crippled, the mute and many others, and laid them at his feet; and he healed them. The people were amazed when they saw the mute speaking, the crippled made well, the lame walking and the blind seeing. And they praised the God of Israel.

So what Jesus *did* is at least as important as what he *said*. He probably did a lot of ordinary things. For all we know, he might have been an excellent cook or an expert outdoorsman. Did he make use of his carpentry skills at all on his travels? We don't hear a lot about the routine things Jesus did. But his life seems chock full of miracles. Maybe that's only because they're so unusual and loom larger than life in our minds. Or maybe it's because with four gospels, we wind up reading them more than once. How many can you actually recall? There's Lazarus, yeah? And a blind guy or two and the "Who touched me?" woman, and . . .

Wait. Let's do this more scientifically. Plow through the gospels. Pull out the miracle stories. Peruse them to pare down duplications. Pop the ones that are left into a spreadsheet. What do you get? A fair number but not what you'd call a lot: about thirty-six altogether. Want a list of them? Nice chart with colors and circles and arrows? You are so in the wrong book, pal.

Thirty-six. If you reckon that Jesus' public ministry was three years long, that gives you a miracle once a month. At that rate, if you were a disciple, hanging with Jesus, nothing spooky would happen for twenty-nine days out of every thirty. Don't call in sick that day!

Except it wasn't like that. Real life doesn't lend itself very well to computerized statistical grids. Most folks count up miracle stories. There are a whole wealth of other passages that didn't make it into the spreadsheet window, passages full of general descriptions about how all kinds of people came to Jesus and he healed them. It seems like there's a constant stream of crowds and healings multi-tasked in a background window (see for example Mark 1:32, 39, 45; 3:10; 6:1–5, 53–56). At least, you and I reading the gospels experience it this way. There are healings of particular people in the foreground and then, somewhere in the background, summaries of crowds of people among whom Jesus worked.

But that's not how the disciples would have lived it. For them, the one-after-anotherness of the crowds would have dominated their attention. It is only later, in telling others about it all, that some individual stories stood out.

Ever work in retail? If so, your day was dominated by one ordinary customer after another. But when you tell people about your job, you summarize whole ordinary weeks in a single sentence and then tell about the one guy who exchanged things eighteen times or the time the credit card machine went crazy or the time that woman came in begowned on her way to her wedding and found the exact thing she was looking for. Your days were dominated by the routine, but your tales and memoirs will be dominated by the rare incidents.

Jesus' ministry by no means depended on miracles. He frequently amazed, delighted or infuriated people without using supernatural surprises. But Jesus' ministry was characterized by miracles. More precisely, it was characterized by healing. That's the first kind of miracle, the kind we find in the multi-tasking backdrop.

The second kind of miracle, what we call "nature miracles", is rarer. That's why you'll find the Twelve not generally surprised by any of Jesus' healings, but frequently astonished or shocked by the nature miracles. Bring a sick guy to Jesus and even the slowest disciple can tell you what's likely to happen. But bring a few fishes and loaves to Jesus and the disciples haven't a clue what will happen next. After the calming of the storm, they ask each other, "What kind of man is this?" (Matt. 8:27) even though they've seen him healing people for months.

During Jesus' life, the healings attracted people to follow him (Matt. 4:25). The writers probably also figured that Jesus' mighty acts authenticated the claims made about him. Ironically, the opposite was true through the twentieth century: miracles became an intellectual barrier to accepting the Bible. Even though quantum physics has demolished the idea that our universe is a closed three-dimensional system of "natural" cause and effect, something of this old-fashioned attitude has carried over into the twenty-first century. So there is, even today, no shortage of people willing to "explain" Jesus' miracles. As I take you through some of the relevant passages later, I'll share some of these rationalizations with you. They're often entertainingly ludicrous.

It is true, though, that we know more about some stuff than the ancients did. But the main thing we're better at is "how". Explaining natural events and then exploiting the principles behind them—that's what we do best.

The ancients who saw birds flying did not think that was a miracle. They even knew that it had something to do with those flappy things on the sides of their bodies. But we can explain how those wings work and use those principles to move beyond wax wings on our arms to sweet little biplanes like the Nieuport 27.

Being so good at the "how" bits gives us a false confidence. If we can see how a thing might work, we accept it works. So far so good. But if we can't see *how*, then we're skeptical about *whether*. And we're often wrong. For most of the twentieth century, scientists were unable to explain how a bumblebee manages to fly. They graciously admitted there was a gap in their understanding, much to the relief of bee-dom in general.

But now imagine you lived on an alternative earth. In this world, hunted for their pelts, bees became extinct in the eighteenth century. Experts in that twentieth century would regard old accounts or drawings of bees in flight as fantastic exaggeration. We might have preserved carcasses, but we'd believe their wings must have been vestigial, like a chicken's. Accounts of their flying must have been written or drawn by uneducated, unscientific people. Such innocent simple-minded folks knew bees had wings, and therefore mistakenly assumed bees could fly, bless 'em. But that's all there is to it: the creatures we know as bumblebees could not have flown. It's all there—do the mathematical calculations yourself if you don't believe us—things of that body mass could not fly with the area and shape of wing that they had! Any evidence to the contrary must be dismissed, even though the myth of bee flight was so appealing that it somehow spread throughout the world and across cultures.

Well, even in our universe, there are lots of things we cannot explain. If they happen frequently, we sometimes graciously own up to imperfect knowledge. But if the thing only happens once or rarely? The accounts of the event are simply discredited. In our universe, scientists kept at the bee-thing until finally they figured out the how. They didn't give up—but only because bees are such in-your-face critters that their flight could not be ignored. If they'd been extinct, there'd have been no reason to keep at it: we'd have proved once and for all that bees cannot fly. This is more or less where the twentieth century has left us with Jesus' miracles. Ancient texts by "simple" people can be swatted to one side more easily than bees. At least in the short term.

Jesus was in the disciples' faces all the time. And he often forced them to reexamine what they thought they knew. They sometimes made and threw away hypotheses as much as any white-coated boffin, as we'll see in our next passage.

Suggestions for Further Thought

One of the most profound changes in Western culture over the past twenty years has been the increased acceptance of spirituality and the supernatural. How do you resolve the tension between having an open mind and not being gullible when you hear of "miracles"?

Think of some people you know who don't believe in Jesus. Are his miracles interesting to them, or are they a barrier?

Walking on Water

When they saw him walking on the lake, they thought he was a ghost.

Mark 6:45–51

Immediately Jesus made his disciples get into the boat and go on ahead of him to Bethsaida, while he dismissed the crowd. After leaving them, he went up on a mountainside to pray.

When evening came, the boat was in the middle of the lake, and he was alone on land. He saw the disciples straining at the oars, because the wind was against them. Shortly before dawn he went out to them, walking on the lake. He was about to pass by them, but when they saw him walking on the lake, they thought he was a ghost. They cried out, because they all saw him and were terrified.

Immediately he spoke to them and said, "Take courage! It is I. Don't be afraid." Then he climbed into the boat with them, and the wind died down. They were completely amazed.

One of the best known of the "nature miracles" is this unusual passage about Jesus walking on water (also found in Matt. 14:22–33 and John 6:16–21). Some of the old-school commentators have tried to rationalize the event away by arguing that Jesus was walking on the beach parallel with the boat, or (get this!) on a sort of natural raft made of reeds in the water, just below the surface where the disciples couldn't see it but parallel to the course of their boat journey.

That kind of explanation was regarded as easier to believe than the accounts based on eyewitness testimony! Here's how sad the modernist era was: people could say that stuff with a straight face.

The disciples' idea that "Jesus' spirit" was coming to them over the water is often used as an example of how naïve and superstitious they were. But the reverse is true. If you're willing to put yourself into the disciples' yamulkas for a few minutes, the whole episode becomes a demonstration of just how knowledgeable they were and how logically and scientifically their minds worked.

They were in the boat, toiling away. Then they saw what looked to them like Jesus, walking to them on the water. Seeing this apparition, what did they make of it? What would you have made of it?

Modern people think they have a good reason for dismissing the biblical evidence. Let's face it, they'll say, the biblical authors were largely uneducated, unenlightened peasants. Back then . . . well, you know . . . they were ignorant of the laws of nature and of scientific methods as we know them now.

This is, of course, half beside the point and half complete nonsense. Ancient people, in their unplugged, nonmotorized world, had an intimate, detailed and deeply practical knowledge of how things worked. Many of these guys were fishermen; they knew more about boats and nets and the sea than most of us will ever know.

If their willingness to accept miracles were simply a matter of not knowing what could and couldn't happen, then they would not have judged the miracles as any more remarkable than anything else. But the gospel writers knew very well the things that Jesus did were contrary to the way the world usually behaved. That's precisely why they called them "miracles".

If the disciples were merely naïve primitives with no conception of the laws of nature, you'd expect them to smile and point stupidly and say, "Look, there's Jesus out for a walk."

But instead, they're terrified; far from thinking it merely unexpected, they've got some idea how extraordinary it is. Their reasoning seems to have gone something like this: Even though that looks like Jesus, we must reckon with the fact that it is able to walk on the water. There's a problem here. We know that Jesus belongs to the set "people", but we also know that things rightly called people cannot walk on water. Therefore, there must be some other explanation. Either he is not really walking on water, or it is not actually

Jesus. You can tell just how sure they were that the thing they saw was actually on the water by the fact that they plump for the alternative. Despite their eyes telling them that it is Jesus, their reason tells them that it must be something else, some kind of thing that has the property of floating upright or something that has properties they don't understand very well. It's too big to be a duck; perhaps it's a "spirit".

Does this sound to you like naïve, unsystematic thinking? On the contrary, the deliberate questioning of the evidence before their very eyes—it looks like Jesus—on the basis of properties they understand Jesus' body to have and not have, shows that they are thinking very "scientifically".

Then, lo and behold, the hypothesis they record is not how it is. Contrary to their expectations, it is Jesus after all. This is not superstition. Superstition would be if the disciples were scared that the spirit of Jesus would come to them, though it never did. Superstition would be if they encountered a storm and were convinced that it was the spirit of Jesus. Superstition does not normally make hypotheses and abandon them.

They proceed in a way that is recognizably scientific and self-critical. It is only their declaration "It must be a spirit we see" that seems to modern people to show the disciples' primitive mind-set.

But this is manifestly unfair of us. It's a carryover from last century when there was a bias against anything supernatural. A twentieth century reader would have been happier with disciples who said, "He must have invented some radical new floatation device." The so-called "scientific worldview" often has surprisingly little to do with evidence and everything to do with what fits in with what we already believe. We often decide ahead of time what phenomena are in the realm of possibility by deciding ahead of time how well the idea conforms to "nature" as we currently think about it. And we slide the scale of what evidence is required on that basis.

The deck is so stacked by our modern framework of thought. Otherwise, we might not have found the thinking of the disciples so naïve after all. They seem to be thinking logically and, at least in terms of method, scientifically. But the important thing is that Jesus shattered their categories as he also shatters ours. He no more conforms to their idea of what was possible than he conforms to our own. Surprise! A guy can walk on water! More maritime mischief in our next passage.

Suggestions for Further Thought

C. S. Lewis wrote about what he called "chronological snobbery"—the conviction that people in times past were more gullible and less clever than we are. How well does this describe your own feelings about the disciples or other historical figures?

Read the story again, trying to imagine yourself as one of the quiet disciples in the boat. The terror and relief will have made this an event you won't quickly forget, but how would that experience have changed you?

Calming the Storm

Jesus was in the stern, sleeping on a cushion.

Mark 4:35–41

That day when evening came, he said to his disciples, "Let us go over to the other side." Leaving the crowd behind, they took him along, just as he was, in the boat. There were also other boats with him. A furious squall came up, and the waves broke over the boat, so that it was nearly swamped. Jesus was in the stern, sleeping on a cushion. The disciples woke him and said to him, "Teacher, don't you care if we drown?"

He got up, rebuked the wind and said to the waves, "Quiet! Be still!" Then the wind died down and it was completely calm.

He said to his disciples, "Why are you so afraid? Do you still have no faith?"

They were terrified and asked each other, "Who is this? Even the wind and the waves obey him!"

The story of Jesus calming the storm is filled with little oddities in all three gospels that tell of it (Matt. 8, Mark 4, Luke 8). It starts innocently, with Jesus wanting to get himself and his disciples to the other side of the Sea of Galilee. Partway across, a storm blew up, as they do in that part of the world. It must have been a pretty ferocious one—many of the disciples were fishermen, and the Sea of Galilee was their home turf (so to speak). They wake Jesus, because he's curled up in the back, sleeping. He then calms the storm and criticizes the disciples ("Where is your faith?" Luke 8:25). They were amazed at his power and asked themselves, "What kind of man is this? Even the winds and waves obey him!" (Matt. 8:27) And they reached the other side. Thus far the text.

The first oddity: why does Jesus criticize the poor old disciples? My Sunday school teachers would be proud of them: if you're in trouble, go and ask Jesus for help. I think it must be that the disciples came to Jesus with an attitude of fear and panic ("Don't you care if we drown?" Mark 4:38 NIV) rather than trust and hope.

But hang on a second, what the heck was he doing asleep in the first place? He was tired and all, but sleeping through a life-threatening storm? This is a little boat; we're not talking about some ocean liner here—"Oh, waiter, could you leave that ice sculpture for a second and knock on the door of Jesus' cabin and ask him to look out of the porthole?"

Now if you and I sometimes sleep well, the perfect Son of God must have been able to sleep flawlessly. Even so, isn't it odd the gospel writers rarely record it? I mean, Jesus must have slept most days, probably took naps at other times, but they never mention it anywhere else.

And another oddity: it would be one thing if a bunch of strangers witnessed Jesus calming the storm and then asked themselves, "Whoa! Who is this guy?" But the *disciples*? Why should *this* miracle cause them to rethink their ideas about Jesus?

You're never going to understand this until you learn something about the ancient Hebrews. They were not a sea-faring nation like, say, the Phoenicians. They're a coastal nation that never had a navy. The sea does not represent trade and opportunity to them. The waters represent Chaos; the sea is the enemy, occasionally personified as a sea monster (Job 7:12; 9:13; 26:12 and Isa. 27:1.) The terror of the sea is reflected in passages such as Jonah 2:3: "You hurled me into the deep, into the very heart of the seas, and the currents swirled about me; all your waves and breakers swept over me."

Psalm 93:4 says God is mightier than the breakers of the sea—it highlights something else that holds throughout the Scriptures. God tends to represent himself through fire: the pillar of fire, the burning bush and so on. But he tends to demonstrate his power by exerting control over waters and the face of the deep. The close of the book of Revelation describes a time when wars cease and God has no more enemies. The author writes: "There was no longer any sea" (Rev. 21:1). So whatever else you were planning to do in the afterlife, get your surfing in now, dude!

If you had to pick the two chunks of the Old Testament most central to the Hebrews' ideas about God and themselves, you would have to pick Creation and Exodus. God's triumph over the water is central to both. In the Creation narrative, the formlessness and chaotic emptiness that existed before God made anything are represented as the deep over which God's Spirit hovers. Reading the story on its own terms, it doesn't look so much as though God created water but more as though he wrestled with it and subdued it. When you or I try to express what it was like before Creation or before the Big Bang, we can't help talking about empty space and blackness, but of course neither of those things would have existed at that point. So with the Hebrews, writing about the pre-Creation. Of course they knew the oceans and waters didn't exist, but the deep was culturally all tied up in the very ideas of Chaos and Disorder and Nothingness.

So the waters are dangerous; the sea is a perilous place, full of terror. Anyone who thinks fishermen like the disciples would regard the sea any other way has never lived in a fishing community. There you will always find a respect for, if not fear of, the deep. Everyone has a relative, a neighbor, a close friend who was taken. And everyone lives with the controlled dread of not knowing who will be the next not to come home.

For the Jewish fishermen disciples, with their religious and cultural background, working the sea was like making a living with high-voltage electricity or at a nuclear energy plant. (I'll leave you to make your own fission/fishin' jokes.)

Now God, when he chooses to speak to people, is willing to use images and methods that will make sense to them. For example, the plagues in the Exodus story are not arbitrary choices: "Let's see, what have we got lying around heaven that I can use on Pharaoh? . . . Oooh, how 'bout frogs!" Each plague confronts one of the Egyptian gods on his/her/its specialty. God adapts to his audiences' fears and understandings. So when God speaks to the Hebrews, it is on a mountaintop; there's smoke and fire. He speaks through those things. But the manifestation of his power in the Exodus account—the central part of the story as far as the Jews are concerned? The parting of the Red Sea. Hey, you who are scared of the sea, this is a God who can wrestle with the waters and win.

Jesus walked on the water; Jesus calmed the stormy sea. These were not ordinary miracles (if I can use that phrase). The disciples may have seen Jesus doing miracles before, making jugs of wine, healing a leper. But Jesus stilling the storm? To the Hebrew mind, that's like Jesus wandering nonchalantly into the reactor core and stopping the Chernobyl disaster with his bare hands. Whoa! What manner of man is this?

That's why this miracle causes his Jewish followers to radically rethink. This goes beyond healing. This puts Jesus in the same sort of lofty category as Moses, but without the wooden staff. The Old Testament promised a future "prophet like Moses", and this is not lost on the gospel writers.

The story is awkward for old-style Jesus Seminar–type scholars who dismiss the gospels as propaganda, the miracles as fictional symbolic statements of Jesus' greatness. Why create a peculiar story with Jesus sleeping? Why muddy the waters (sorry) with a subplot in which disciples (the church leadership of the writers) are shown in a bad light? And most of all, if you want to create a story to show Jesus as a "prophet like Moses", if you want to give the disciples a reason to be amazed, why not have this Jesus who wants to get to the other side of the sea part the waters for himself and the disciples to walk through?

The disciples were amazed at this miracle. And although they must have had a pretty high opinion of their Lord before this, in the face of these waves and these winds, it was Jesus who totally blew them away. Time for a reevaluation. "Who is this guy?" That's exactly what Jesus wants them to be thinking. It's not long till he'll be asking them for the results of this rethink: "Who do you say I am?"

Suggestions for Further Thought

If this story is not about the weather but about Jesus' supremacy over Chaos, that probably has a lot more relevance to our lives. Take a few minutes and imagine Jesus waking up and confronting the Chaos in your life.

Maybe mastery over water doesn't do it for you the way it did for the disciples. Has there ever been a time in your life when you looked at something God has done and marveled, "What kind of God is this?"

The Fig Tree

They saw the fig tree withered from the roots.

Mark 11:12–20

The next day as they were leaving Bethany, Jesus was hungry. Seeing in the distance a fig tree in leaf, he went to find out if it had any fruit. When he reached it, he found nothing but leaves, because it was not the season for figs. Then he said to the tree, "May no one ever eat fruit from you again." And his disciples heard him say it.

On reaching Jerusalem, Jesus entered the temple courts and began driving out those who were buying and selling there. He overturned the tables of the money changers and the benches of those selling doves, and would not allow anyone to carry merchandise through the temple courts. And as he taught them, he said, "Is it not written: 'My house will be called a house of prayer for all nations'? But you have made it 'a den of robbers.'"

The chief priests and the teachers of the law heard this and began looking for a way to kill him, for they feared him, because the whole crowd was amazed at his teaching.

When evening came, Jesus and his disciples went out of the city.

In the morning, as they went along, they saw the fig tree withered from the roots.

All the nature miracles seem to be about either big bodies of water or catering. Here's one where Jesus whacks the first century equivalent of a Coke machine that swallowed his coins. Except that when Jesus whacks a Coke machine, it winds up as a smoking heap of twisted metal. This miracle may qualify as Jesus' weirdest.

Okay, okay, I lied. As you read in the passage, it wasn't really a Coke machine. On his way to Jerusalem with the disciples, Jesus went to check out a lush, leafy fig tree. Finding no fruit there, he cursed the tree, which then withered incredibly quickly, so the next time they looked at it, it was dead. Deceased. It was an ex-tree.

The commentaries on this passage reach their most impenetrably boring on what was and wasn't the season for figs. In one way it's amusing to watch theologians try to sound like competent botanists. They're busy sprinkling original Aramaic terms into discussions about which trees bear which kind of fruit in which months of the Jewish calendar. Riveting. But if you trust these guys to have done their homework, it turns out that an ancient Israelite would expect a crop of unpleasant but edible "early figs" that all drop off before the main crop comes. You can imagine the metaphorical use that all this is put to, but the real fun is in what comes next.

Many people read Mark 11:14 without noticing how peculiar it is: "Then he said to the tree, 'May no one ever eat fruit from you again.'" The learned people are all arguing about whether this was a "curse" or a "pronouncement" or what. Hang on a minute . . . never mind what he said. Look at to whom he said it. "Then he said to the tree"—to the tree?! Are the disciples standing there wondering about the technical differences between curse and pronouncement formulae? I don't think so. They're thinking, *Oh, great, we're heading into the most delicate political situation of our lives and the Boss is picking a fight with the plant life!*

Matthew says that the tree withered "right away", but Mark is more specific. It didn't take a season or a week, but by the next day it was withered right to its roots. The little sprouts of grass in my driveway I dose with weed killer every year take longer than that. What power!

That's another strange thing. This is Jesus' only purely negative miracle, the only miracle of destruction. The gospels love to show Jesus as a powerful guy, but they usually do so without any explosions or smash-bang car chases.

Those are the definitions of power I'm used to in my literature—Ben Grimm of the Fantastic Four smashing boulders with his bare orange hands! Kaboom! It's clobbering time!

The rare exceptions to the power-equals-destruction equation have always fascinated me: the superhero Green Lantern (Hal Jordan in his pre-Specter days) once used his power ring to catch bad guys in a giant green force-field ice cream scoop. Jesus is usually portrayed in this more creative, nondestructive mold. The only other Jesus story that comes anywhere close to lethal is in Mark 5, the incident about the daredevil kamikaze pigs. But the loss of the herd off the cliff was only a side effect—the main thrust of the miracle was a positive event. And it might not have been reckoned such a disaster anyway, since pigs are unclean for Jews.

But why zap a poor defenseless fig tree? Fig trees aren't even the bad guys. Fig trees are good upstanding citizens. In fact, figs and fig trees are used in the Scriptures as a symbol for Israel itself. (See Jer. 24; 29:17; Hos. 9:10; Mic. 7:1–6; and to a lesser extent, Isa. 34:4; Jer. 5:17; 8:13; Hos. 2:12; Joel 1:7, 12. Convinced yet?) Nor was this some renegade evil fig tree roving around the countryside committing random acts of violence or harboring figs of mass destruction. Its crime was that it had no figs when it wasn't even the season for figs.

So if the tree was minding its own business, why did he biff it?

I think Mark's gospel tells us the answer, although in an unexpected way. Bear with me here as I go into academic mode. Several times in his gospel, Mark will stick two stories together. It's like bookends or a sandwich—Mark starts with story 1, leaves it unfinished, then flits to story 2 before returning to resolve story 1 on the other end. Bread . . . meat . . . bread again. And when Mark does this, it's a good bet that the interrupted story 1 and story 2 in the middle are meant to help explain each other. In our passage, the fig tree is story 1, the rye bread, and it's got plenty of mustard:

1—(beginning) Jesus and the boys encounter the fig tree on their way to Jerusalem.

2—Then comes a different story.

1—(ending) Then, the next day, they see the fig tree withered.

So if we get the meaning of story 2, we may get the meaning of the fig tree. But what is the pastrami? What is story 2?

The mystery story is the one in which Jesus enters the temple and chases the dove sellers and money changers right out of there. This is Herod's refurbished temple, the place about which the disciples themselves exclaimed in Mark 13:1, "What massive stones! What magnificent buildings!" The temple cleansing and the fig tree cursing are related. Remember that the fig tree had already been used as a symbol for Israel. And in Jesus' day the temple was a magnificent symbol of Israel's religious dedication. Remember too that Jesus found the fig tree magnificent with leaves but with no fruit. Hmmm. When he spoke to the fig tree, was it for the benefit of the tree or the disciples?

Aha. This miracle has less to do with hunger and seasons than it does with symbolic teaching. Again, the Old Testament prophets provide some of the background to things like this. Lots of them went around teaching not only by telling parables but sometimes by acting them out. That's sure to be what's going on here: an acted parable. Both John the Baptist and Jesus have announced that the kingdom of God is "at hand". It's almost the season: Micah 7:1, "My soul desires the first ripe fig." But there is no real fruit, only the appearance of life in the leaves. Business seems to be booming in the beautiful, newly modernized temple. But are the people truly in relationship with God? Or is it all money mongering and pigeon purchasing?

And in our religion?

Suggestions for Further Thought

Everybody wants growth in their church . . . but how do you tell whether you're growing fruit or just leaves?

I sometimes think if I had been given the job of writing the script for Jesus, I would have had him encourage the poor little tree: "Hey, you're doing a great job with those leaves, but come on now, try a bit harder and produce some fruit to match." Jesus' coming isn't only about love and acceptance; his love seems to include judgement. How do you resolve the tension?

Supper for Thousands

They all ate and were satisfied.

Luke 9:12–17

Late in the afternoon the Twelve came to him and said, "Send the crowd away so they can go to the surrounding villages and countryside and find food and lodging, because we are in a remote place here."

He replied, "You give them something to eat."

They answered, "We have only five loaves of bread and two fish—unless we go and buy food for all this crowd." (About five thousand men were there.)

But he said to his disciples, "Have them sit down in groups of about fifty each." The disciples did so, and everyone sat down. Taking the five loaves and the two fish and looking up to heaven, he gave thanks and broke them. Then he gave them to the disciples to set before the people. They all ate and were satisfied, and the disciples picked up twelve basketfuls of broken pieces that were left over.

This food miracle is the best known of all of them. It is recorded in all four gospels. You'll find it in Matthew 14:14–21; Mark 6:31–44; Luke 9:11–17 and John 6:1–13. What does it mean? Is there, as with the fig tree, an element of the acted parable? Is there some message lurking underneath this story of Jesus' compassion and power?

Some people think the meaning is linked to a non-miraculous "scientific" interpretation. It goes like this: John tells us that the five loaves and two fish belonged not to the disciples but to a small boy. At the Jesus Show that day, many folks brought snacks with them, though many others did not. Jesus decided to use the boy as an object lesson to shame the "haves" into sharing with the "have nots" as this lad did. And, the story goes, when everyone there did that, they were surprised to find that they not only had enough but had several basketfuls left over! There is therefore no miracle, except the miracle of teaching people to share.

But, of course, if that were really what went on, the gospel writers would not have hesitated to say so. The sentiment fits in perfectly with Luke in particular. He's very interested in anything having to do with poverty or wealth and the redistribution thereof. If it were a story about sharing what you have, he'd be sure to have made more of that theme here, just as he does about the early church and their willingness to share the little they had at the end of chapters 2 and 4 of Acts.

Can anyone honestly believe that the gospel writers did not realize that people were sharing with each other rather than Jesus performing a miracle? I don't think so.

Rather, you'd have to believe that the gospel writers magnified the importance of things Jesus did with symbolic significance and, where possible, with a miraculous tint. But a serious reading of the gospels shows this isn't the case either. There are plenty of stories about the unsupernatural things that Jesus did that were still remarkable—his amazing answer to the trap about Caesar's taxes, for instance, or the story about his defusing the mob ready to stone the woman caught in adultery. He is not portrayed as commanding and changing the stones to handfuls of Styrofoam peanuts; he is shown instead as one who spoke and changed people's minds (John 8:1–11). Why leave that story alone and elevate this one into a miracle when doing so destroys the "Everyone should share" moral?

Nope, for the gospel writers, this was a miracle. So if it's not about sharing, what is it about? Be careful when you ask yourself a question like this. We think there has to be some lesson or teaching of which the story is an illustration, like a fable. At the end you can boil it all down to a phrase like "And the moral of the story is: be nice to people and they'll be nice to you." But not all life-changing teaching is like that.

There are two subtly different possibilities. Was Jesus selecting miracles, like parables, to get across a moral or proverb ("It's nice to be nice")? Or was Jesus revealing himself and his character through the miracles? You know me well enough by now to guess my answer. I think they weren't an arbitrary illustration of the truth as much as a case in point. He judged the fig tree because he is the judge; because he is the supplier of good things, he fed the 5,000.

Think about that for a second, though: more than 5,000 live, swarming people. Maybe it's obvious, but that's a lot of people if you're thinking of trying to speak to them without amplification. What's the largest crowd you've ever addressed?

Now, what's the largest party you've ever cooked for? On your own? Spur of the moment?

Feel the worry, then panic, that must have seized the disciples. They're not being faithless; they're coming with a sane warning. For a prophet, they'll have found Jesus remarkably lacking in foresight. Lucky for him, they're thinking ahead, heading off a potentially dangerous situation. "Wind the seminar up, Jesus; the crowd'll need to get home; traffic jams on the road, don't want a mob of 5,000 plus getting cranky with hunger." And Jesus turns to them and asks, "How about if *you* give them something to eat?"

"Who? Me?"

They scrape together a few loaves and fishes. These are not French bread batons and clear packs of smoked salmon. They are not coming to him with some hope that if they can just slice these long loaves thinly enough and spread the cream cheese carefully . . . We're talking a few oval pita breads and part of a tin of sardines. A single disciple, even a small disciple, could have held this banquet in two hands—don't forget how it got out here to begin with: one boy carried all of it and a thermos in his "Go Maccabees!" lunch box. The disciples show the food to Jesus in order to demonstrate there's no way this is gonna work.

But Jesus takes this handful of food. And he does something that becomes characteristic of Jesus at suppers: he takes it, he gives thanks, he breaks it and he gives it out.

I would have loved the chance to watch this. I'd love to know when it starts multiplying. The people sit in groups; the disciples presumably bring food around to them. There are at least twelve of them, and Jesus has broken the bread and fish. Does each server start out with only a half a pita bread and a smidgeon of fish? And as each of the groups passes it around, they find no matter how much bread they tear off this piece, it doesn't get smaller? Somewhere along the way it actually winds up increasing, since the amount of fragments gathered afterwards exceeds the amount we started with. I'd love to know, but we're not told.

The "how" of it—even the wonder of it—isn't really the point. The way that Jesus acts with the bread and fishes in this story is just like the Lord's Supper and the story of the disciples on the road to Emmaus. There are four verbs: he takes the food, gives thanks, breaks it and gives it out. Commentators argue about whether this is meant to remind us of the Lord's Supper. That doesn't go far enough.

Rather, as we'll see later when we discuss the Last Supper, these actions are central to the whole purpose of who and what Jesus was, for all the occasions on which he did this are examples of what is true about Jesus: he is the one who took something up, gave thanks and allowed it to be broken and given out for the good of others. John's gospel, characteristically, spells this all out in much more detail. After feeding the 5,000 in John 6:1–13, Jesus explains to the disciples how he himself is the bread that he will give out (6:25–59). And this is a meal that will satisfy!

In the ancient world even more than today, a person's actions spoke about their character. The miracles shout the character of Jesus: the one who comes to us in whatever boat we're in, no matter what the obstacles; the one who judges; the one who supplies all good things and who gives himself. In the next few passages, we'll see him in one of his favorite roles: the one who restores people and makes them whole again.

Suggestions for Further Thought

Why doesn't Jesus just feed everyone, even today? When you work out the answer to this one, drop me a line c/o Zondervan. Thanks.

Reflect on our role as disciples today. Isn't it similar? Taking little bits that fit into our hands and reaching out as if we believe that these fragments will feed all those people. . .

Ol' Blind Bart & Co.

A blind man, Bartimaeus (which means "son of Timaeus"), was sitting by the roadside begging. When he heard that it was Jesus of Nazareth, he began to shout, "Jesus, Son of David, have mercy on me!" Many rebuked him and told him to be quiet.

Mark 10:46–52

Then they came to Jericho. As Jesus and his disciples, together with a large crowd, were leaving the city, a blind man, Bartimaeus (which means "son of Timaeus"), was sitting by the roadside begging. When he heard that it was Jesus of Nazareth, he began to shout, "Jesus, Son of David, have mercy on me!"

Many rebuked him and told him to be quiet, but he shouted all the more, "Son of David, have mercy on me!"

Jesus stopped and said, "Call him."

So they called to the blind man, "Cheer up! On your feet! He's calling you." Throwing his cloak aside, he jumped to his feet and came to Jesus.

"What do you want me to do for you?" Jesus asked him.

The blind man said, "Rabbi, I want to see."

"Go," said Jesus, "your faith has healed you." Immediately he received his sight and followed Jesus along the road.

The New Testament contains some pretty weird healings, and I'll tell you about the most bizarre shortly. By contrast, the healing of Bartimaeus is reassuringly children's-sermonic. One day, Jesus and a crowd of hangers-on are out strolling right past Bartimaeus, who is begging. He, naturally, can't see what's going on but can sense the excitement. So somebody punches him a quick memo in Braille: "It's Jesus of Naoareth" (missed a dot in that z—easily done). And immediately, Bart is all, "Jesus, Son of David, have mercy on me!" Don't you wonder how he knows about Jesus and his ancestry? Jesus' reputation must be pretty well established in this place.

The crowds in Mark are usually involved in bringing the sick people to Jesus' attention. But not this crew; they tell Bartimaeus to be quiet. Why? It's not that they dislike him or are nonvisually prejudiced, for once Jesus stops and calls for him, they rise to the occasion: "Cheer up! On your feet! He's calling you." It looks as though the crowd isn't so much preventing him from bothering the Master as wanting him to avoid using that charged political title "Son of David (the king)" in public. Shhh!

But Jesus calls, and Bart's response is something that has delighted preachers ever since. A beggar, yet he throws aside his cloak; a man sitting forlornly by the roadside, yet he jumps to his feet; a blind person, yet he rushes toward the sound of the voice that called him. "Oops, 'scuse me." "Ouch!" "Pardon me." "Oh, sorry 'bout that." Jesus doesn't always require such an approach, but he must have loved it.

As an aside, I wonder what the apostle Paul made of this story. Jesus called him on a road as well. Only Jesus took his sight away rather than giving it to him (Acts 9)!

Anyway, Bartimaeus made his way to Jesus, who asked, "What do you want me to do for you?" Folks like me, full of attitude and wisecracks, have a lot to learn from Bartimaeus's simplicity and clarity. "Rabbi, I want to see." Hey, just the fact that he doesn't get angry at the question is a lesson.

Then comes a famous phrase of Jesus': "Go, your faith has healed you." Of course, it isn't his faith that has done it . . . at least not in the new-agey "Just see yourself healed and it'll happen" sort of way. It is Jesus who has healed him, and somehow the thing that allowed it to happen is Bartimaeus's faith in Jesus (rather than in healing).

In both Mark and Luke, the healing looks as though it was accomplished merely with a word of Jesus. Matthew 20, however, adds the details about a second blind man (Bartimaeus is so exemplary that one can readily understand Mark's streamlining) and that Jesus touched his eyes as part of the healing.

In some of the other blind guy stories, he does more than that. In Mark 8, Jesus spits in another guy's eyes and then puts his hands on him. John's narrative of the man born blind in chapter 9 is, if you can believe it, even more gross. Jesus "spit on the ground, made some mud with the saliva, and put it on the man's eyes" (v. 6).

Yeah, right. If he can heal with a word or mere touch, why did he sometimes go through all this rigmarole of spit and mud?

Let me answer by telling you about a truly bizarre miracle, as promised. Luke introduces this incident in the city of Ephesus by saying, "God did extraordinary miracles" (Acts 19:11). What a great phrase. Extraordinary miracles! As if there are ordinary, garden-variety, generic-brand miracles. It is extraordinary, though: we're told that handkerchiefs and aprons used by Paul were taken around Ephesus and people were healed of illnesses just by touching them. The Bible has no comparable stories about Jesus! Why does God do these magic-object miracles through Paul?

The better question is, I think, why does he do them in Ephesus? Have a look at Acts 19 sometime: in Ephesus sorcerers went around using magical formulae to combat evil spirits. In Ephesus the converts burnt their magical scrolls. Ephesus was a city obsessed with magical power. And in Ephesus, God worked extraordinary magic-like miracles. The other extreme was the Greek city of Athens. That was a city not bewitched with magic but under the spell of philosophy. Acts 17 tells us of Paul's famous speech there, in which he quoted Greek thinkers and writers. But as far as we know, he did no miracles in Athens. Coincidence?

I don't think so. Instead, I've taken this as a clue to read back into the gospels. In some of his healings, Jesus just waves his hands and heals at a distance: folks start off home only to find that their loved ones started feeling better the exact hour Jesus said they would. In other cases, he goes through elaborate procedures that we find strange, as with the deaf and mute guy who gets his tongue spat on and his ear holes tapped while Jesus looks up to heaven and intones, "Ephphatha!" (Mark 7:33–34). Then again, maybe it's not so odd . . . try speaking Aramaic without spitting! *Ephphatha*, indeed! (By the way, did you know that the Greek word meaning "to spit" is *ptuo*? Aren't ancient languages cool?)

The reason for all this variety has to do not with the healer but with the person being healed. Jesus started with people where they were at, in order to take them further. To the philosophers, the first contact looks a little like philosophy; to the magicians, the first contact looks a little like magical powers. So it's not that Jesus needed the mud in order for the healing to take place, or that damaged retinas respond to the silicate in certain types of clay when amino acids from saliva are introduced as a catalyst. Instead, the blind man may have needed these props in order to relate to what was about to happen. It looks as though the few incidents in which Jesus healed at a distance are precisely the incidents in which the people asking had exemplary faith. (See Matt. 8:5–13 and 15:21–28. In the case of the official's son, John 4:46–53, Jesus' harsh words are directed at the crowd, in contrast to the man who has taken him at his word). Hmm . . . we seem to have arrived back at the question of the relationship between faith and healing.

But before we move to the next encounter to look at that more closely, notice, please, the difference between our notions of medical practice and how Jesus works. He tailors his actions to the person, not to the illness or symptom. Jesus doesn't say, "Oh, blindness, eh? I know that one: that's a spitter. Stand still, big guy; *ptuo*!" It's not just blindness either. Compare stories of fevers or paralysis or even revived dead folks, and sometimes Jesus touches them, sometimes takes their hands; sometimes it's just his words that do it. Isn't this interesting: we concentrate on the illness and endeavour to standardize the treatment regardless of who needs it. Jesus does the reverse, I think. When confronting folks with medical complaints, his method and mechanics of treatment are tailored not to the illness but to the person.

Suggestions for Further Thought

If I'm right about Ephesus and Athens, what styles of mission would be the most appropriate for your culture and subculture?

In what ways are you like Bartimaeus? What risks has he taken to get to Jesus, and what risks should you be taking?

The Ungrateful Paralytic

So they asked him, "Who is this fellow who told you to pick it up and walk?" The man who was healed had no idea.

John 5:1–16

Some time later, Jesus went up to Jerusalem for one of the Jewish festivals. Now there is in Jerusalem near the Sheep Gate a pool, which in Aramaic is called Bethesda and which is surrounded by five covered colonnades. Here a great number of disabled people used to lie—the blind, the lame, the paralyzed. One who was there had been an invalid for thirty-eight years. When Jesus saw him lying there and learned that he had been in this condition for a long time, he asked him, "Do you want to get well?"

"Sir," the invalid replied, "I have no one to help me into the pool when the water is stirred. While I am trying to get in, someone else goes down ahead of me."

Then Jesus said to him, "Get up! Pick up your mat and walk." At once the man was cured; he picked up his mat and walked.

The day on which this took place was a Sabbath, and so the Jewish leaders said to the man who had been healed, "It is the Sabbath; the law forbids you to carry your mat."

But he replied, "The man who made me well said to me, 'Pick up your mat and walk.'"

So they asked him, "Who is this fellow who told you to pick it up and walk?"

The man who was healed had no idea who it was, for Jesus had slipped away into the crowd that was there.

Later Jesus found him at the temple and said to him, "See, you are well again. Stop sinning or something worse may happen to you." The man went away and told the Jewish leaders that it was Jesus who had made him well.

So, because Jesus was doing these things on the Sabbath, the Jewish leaders began to persecute him.

There's much in the gospels to encourage us to think that faith is a prerequisite for miracles, especially healings. The idea that the people with the greatest faith need fewer "props" is just one strand of this rope. Another is the saying we looked at earlier: "Your faith has healed you." Still another is the curious account of Jesus' visit to a village in Mark 6:5–6: "He could not do any miracles there, except lay his hands on a few sick people and heal them. He was amazed at their lack of faith." Matthew 13:58 clarifies this slightly as, "And he did not do many miracles there because of their lack of faith." Mark's wording allows the reader to get the idea that the lack of faith presents a barrier to Jesus doing his stuff, like kryptonite to Superman (except that, oh yeah, he did heal a few people! Some barrier!). Matthew has removed the ambiguity in the wording—"did not do" rather than "could not do"—but still leaves us with the impression that Jesus looked for faith before deciding whether to do a miracle or not.

But wait, faith isn't always mentioned in the healing passages. Maybe it's there and the writer assumes it rather than spells it out? Does the fact that a person was willing to stand up or stretch out their arms or whatever at Jesus' command imply some kind of faith and trust in him? It isn't hard to find preachers who tell you that if you want to be healed, you have to have faith, and if you don't have faith, you won't be healed. So, by implication, if you're not healed, it must be due to a lack in your faith.

You don't have to think very hard or read very far before you realize that it isn't quite that simple. It cannot be just that sometimes the faith isn't mentioned but assumed. On occasion, the passage mentions the faith of the people who brought the sick person to Jesus rather than the faith of the person to be healed. So you don't need to have faith; you just need to have someone plead for you who does! In that case, if you're not healed, maybe it's the church's fault! In the gospels, sometimes the person being healed not only doesn't have faith, but doesn't even have consciousness; sometimes they don't even have a pulse!

Let me remind you of this story you've just read in which everyone's eyes are open, yet nobody has any faith. If the Bible was intending to teach that faith is necessary, here's an occasion when Jesus would have told the guy, "Forget it, man!" There's this paralyzed guy, lying in a place called the Bethesda Sheep Gate, near a pool. The people believe that when the pool bubbles up, the waters will heal you of whatever ails you. So it becomes the hangout for the down-and-outs. All kinds of disabled people are there waiting for the bubbles, waiting to get lucky. Enter Jesus. He goes up to one guy who's been paralyzed for nearly forty years and asks him, "Do you want to get well?"

Remember that good guys in the gospel answer simply. Not this Joe. He falls back on negativity: blaming other people and begrudging others. "Nobody helps me into the water when it's time, and some other selfish so-and-so always gets there ahead of me." Can't you just hear the acidity in his voice? As if he wouldn't barge in there ahead of the others if he had the chance. I think the gospel writer is deliberately showing this guy in a bad light.

Jesus heals him anyway. There's a whole crowd of disabled folks there; surely some had more faith than this? Jesus picks out this guy—John doesn't tell us that Jesus healed anyone else, and the way the story unfolds with the Pharisees, it seems unlikely anyone else was healed. "Get up! Pick up your mat and walk." And the man does.

Are we meant to take that as an expression of faith? I don't think so. Look how the story continues. The guy walks out of there carrying his bed and the Sabbath-cop Pharisees book him for unauthorized carrying of slumber furniture in a Day of Rest zone. What does our healed dude do? Is he reformed? Nope. Just as before, his first impulse is to say that it's all someone else's fault, this time Jesus'. "Carrying the bed wasn't my idea, Officer. The guy who healed me told me to do this." Only he hasn't even bothered to find out Jesus' name. "Who is this fellow who told you to pick it up and walk?" they ask him. The gospel tells us that he was clueless. Some faith!

Does he go back and try to find Jesus to thank him properly? No way. Instead Jesus finds him later and delivers a chilling message: "See, you are well again. Stop sinning or something worse may happen to you." But, heedless, once the man finds out who it is that's healed him, he goes straight back to the authorities and rats on Jesus. I'm telling you, this guy is a nasty piece of work. He's sneering and grimacing in both the before and after photos.

Is there faith here? Is Jesus after the kind of faith that stands up on command and then does the sorts of things this guy does? I can't buy that.

If anything, it seems more likely that Jesus intends the healing to be a catalyst in this guy's life, to help him change. "Look, you're healed; now get the rest of your act together before something worse happens."

Even the method of healing points to this catalyst role for the healing. In the previous "encounter", we said that Jesus starts where people are in order to take them further. Jesus is willing to use props in healings, but not this time. He could have conformed to the guy's expectations and used the pool, bubbling or not, but he heals with a word instead. Here even the healing is an attempt to take the man further.

So is faith the precondition? Or is faith the desired outcome? Are the miracles about us and our maimed condition? Or are they about him? Our next story is an unusual one that may help answer these questions.

Suggestions for Further Thought

Compare this guy with Blind Bartimaeus. When things go wrong, who are you more like?

We love to hear Jesus' tender promises. But his chilling message is not one that the paralytic wanted to hear any more than we'd want to. Is it aimed at us as well, though? Look, you are well now. Stop sinning or something worse may happen to you.

The Reverse Roofers

"Which is easier: to say, 'Your sins are forgiven,' or to say, 'Get up and walk'? But I want you to know that the Son of Man has authority on earth to forgive sins."

Luke 5:17–26

One day Jesus was teaching, and Pharisees and teachers of the law were sitting there. They had come from every village of Galilee and from Judea and Jerusalem. And the power of the Lord was with Jesus to heal the sick. Some men came carrying a paralyzed man on a mat and tried to take him into the house to lay him before Jesus. When they could not find a way to do this because of the crowd, they went up on the roof and lowered him on his mat through the tiles into the middle of the crowd, right in front of Jesus.

When Jesus saw their faith, he said, "Friend, your sins are forgiven."

The Pharisees and the teachers of the law began thinking to themselves, "Who is this fellow who speaks blasphemy? Who can forgive sins but God alone?"

Jesus knew what they were thinking and asked, "Why are you thinking these things in your hearts? Which is easier: to say, 'Your sins are forgiven,' or to say, 'Get up and walk'? But I want you to know that the Son of Man has authority on earth to forgive sins." So he said to the paralyzed man, "I tell you, get up, take your mat and go home." Immediately he stood up in front of them, took what he had been lying on and went home praising God. Everyone was amazed and gave praise to God. They were filled with awe and said, "We have seen remarkable things today."

ere's another paralyzed guy story. You'll know this one if you've ever been in any church program for kids—you've made the little house with the hole in the top and used a cardboard winch to lower the stretcher. It's in three of the four gospels, but it's best put in Luke 5 and Mark 2. (Matthew 9 politely fails to mention some of the creative vandalism.) The story is that some gang wanted to bring their paralyzed buddy to be healed by Jesus. But there was such a crowd that they were unable to get through to where Jesus was. "'Scuse me. Paralyzed guy coming through!" No dice. So they do what any upstanding group of Christians would do: they deface someone else's property. They go up on the roof (not difficult with those houses), dig through it and then lower their mate's mat down in front of Jesus.

What a great day to be a disciple with a sense of humor. Imagine being in that room listening to Jesus. Maybe he said something about his heavenly Father with a sweep of his arm skyward. You inadvertently look up and suddenly some ceiling plaster falls on you and a bit of sky becomes visible.

Or think of this story from the point of view of the guy who owned that house, as in a sermon someone told me about. You can just see it, can't you? It's not all that funny from the owner's perspective. Poor guy hears of this amazing rabbi who can change water into wine, invites him over to his house and winds up with a ruined ceiling instead of an enhanced cellar.

In the face of stories like these, how anyone can believe the authors of the gospels were writing propaganda is beyond me. What propagandist would make this story up, then or now? Can you imagine any church minister you know, or any other Christian leader, condoning the actions of these vandals, much less rewarding them? At least in the West, I think we're probably more concerned to respect personal property than to reward the search for spiritual and physical health. But this is the Jesus who told the parable about selling everything to obtain the pearl of great value (Matt. 13:44–46) and the parable we find so difficult about the shrewd but slightly dishonest financial manager (Luke 16:1–9). He recognizes their single-minded pursuit of restoration for their friend. And all three gospels preface Jesus' actions with the phrase "when he saw their faith".

For the gospel writers, the exchange that happens next is really the main point of the story. Instead of simply healing the paralyzed guy, Jesus uses the occasion to provoke a scene with the Pharisees and teachers of the law, who were probably already objecting to the whole roof business. Jesus sees the friends' faith and, rather than healing straight off, forgives the guy's sins. Jesus' opponents and the house owner are bound to be angered by this. Imagine some guest at your house telling another guest not to worry about a few broken windows. "Who can intervene and forgive all a person's sins but God alone? Who does this Jesus think he is?" And they, of course, will not believe that his sins have actually been forgiven, whatever this Jesus character said. If the paralytic and his pals are gullible enough to believe it, that's just too bad—they'll still be held accountable.

What Jesus does next is astonishing. Whether by miraculous mind reading or ordinary face reading, he can tell what the skeptics are thinking, and he calls them on it: "Which is easier: to say, 'Your sins are forgiven,' or to say, 'Get up and walk'?"

Whoa. What a question to hit the religious establishment with. Now, on the one hand, they should believe that healing is within the realm of humans to tinker with, whereas sins are not. On the other, faced with a real person with a real physical problem, it's much easier to say something about the invisible internal state than to remedy the outward and obvious problem.

Jesus' next sentence is left incomplete in the Greek (although the TNIV translation tidies it up). It's a sentence that surprised me because it implies his motive in healing is to demonstrate something else. Jesus says to his opponents, "But in order that you might know that the Son of Man has authority on earth to forgive sins . . ." The text of all three accounts leaves that dangling as he turns to the paralyzed man again and tells him to get up, pick up his stuff and go home. Naturally, the guy does.

The dangling sentence means that the healing was done not purely for its own sake but almost as a proof of Jesus' authority to those there who were not inclined to recognize it. Again, clearly, the miracles are sometimes about provoking faith in places where Jesus doesn't find it rather than always about responding to faith where he does. We've said the healings are not primarily about the illnesses; now we see they're not even primarily about the person being healed. They are about Jesus and about people's response to and awareness of him. John's gospel quite deliberately refers to all the miracles as signs: real things functioning as pointers, bite-size versions of something else, something much larger. John is on to something there.

But here's a detail I never noticed till just now: The healed guy goes home, and he doesn't go back up through the roof. The crowds that blocked the reverse roofer gang are still there, but it must be that they make room for him now, staring, mouths agape, backing up almost unconsciously to give him space to walk through the midst of them. Meanwhile, I bet the friends back up on the roof are giving each other high fives and jumping up and down, trying to avoid falling in. And Jesus' opponents? Were they convinced?

Suggestions for Further Thought

In other places, Jesus refuses to give a miraculous sign that he is who he says. Why is this case different?

The stakes were pretty high for this paralyzed man and his friends. If you had been in this situation and Jesus had left it at forgiving your friend's sin rather than also healing him, how would you have felt?

Power Outage

Someone touched me.

Luke 8:42-48

As Jesus was on his way, the crowds almost crushed him. And a woman was there who had been subject to bleeding for twelve years, but no one could heal her. She came up behind him and touched the edge of his cloak, and immediately her bleeding stopped.

"Who touched me?" Jesus asked.

When they all denied it, Peter said, "Master, the people are crowding and pressing against you."

But Jesus said, "Someone touched me; I know that power has gone out from me."

Then the woman, seeing that she could not go unnoticed, came trembling and fell at his feet. In the presence of all the people, she told why she had touched him and how she had been instantly healed. Then he said to her, "Daughter, your faith has healed you. Go in peace."

ere's another strange story. When Matthew retells it in 9:19–22, he smoothes out the rough edges. A woman who is ill comes up and touches Jesus, thinking that touching him will heal her. Jesus turns around and sees her. He then encourages her to take heart and tells her that her faith has healed her. And from that encounter, she is healed. The versions in Mark and Luke explain why he has to encourage her: she was hoping to touch him and, once healed, slink away unnoticed. In Jewish society, her disease means she is unclean. She should not be out in public, especially not in a crowd. Everyone is pressed up against everyone else—a touch from her renders *you* unclean.

That's one rough bit Matthew has smoothed over. Of course, it's no real problem for us to note that the woman has a naïve and superstitious belief about touching his garments healing her. The problem is she's right. She brushes the very edge of those bathrobe thingies that Jesus wore and that does the trick. Her bleeding stops. He's still facing the other way, she reaches out and—*whoomph*—she's healed. Magic!

Are you comfortable with this? I'm not.

And it gets worse. Jesus seems to confirm a magical energy thing when he tells the disciples that he felt power go out of him. He needs some serious insulation—a rubber robe would stop that kind of "outflow via outfit". But look at this again: how does he know that power has gone out of him? Has he got virtual power gauges? Whoa—the needles suddenly swing violently into the red for a second—what was that? Who touched me?

The image you might get from this story is of a walking, talking battery full of magical energy that can be released by merely touching him, though not without him knowing it. But is that what Jesus or the gospel writers are trying to tell you? Take note, for this is important and a lesson I'm still learning and wrestling with through this book. Whether our questions are about how miracles work or what we should do about some situation in our personal lives, if we come to the text and all we're concerned about are our questions, we stand an excellent chance of misreading the text. Most of us wouldn't dream of doing this with a friend in person. "Never mind about your problems, here's what *I* want to know." You have to approach the Bible wondering about its questions and interests before learning how to apply them to your own.

You know from the previous encounters that I don't believe there's anything wrong with being curious about the how of the miracles. I'm as curious as anyone about how the things actually worked. But we must remain conscious that the how is not what the authors are writing about, nor is it Jesus' focus.

Remember the Athens-Ephesus thing from our discussion of the blind guys? There are different methods of healing for different people, starting where they are in order to take them further. Look at our story in that light and it all falls into place perfectly.

The woman has the naïve superstitious faith that Jesus is so great that even touching his clothes can heal her. Is she right? Not exactly, but it's as good a place to start as we're going to get. So she's healed according to her expectations. But she's not left there. Verse 47 is every bit as traumatic to her as the healing thing itself. Look how emotional and public! For an unclean female who risked touching her neighbors and making them unclean, to become thus the center of attention must have been terrifying. "Then the woman, seeing that she could not go unnoticed, came trembling and fell at his feet. In the presence of all the people, she told why she had touched him and how she had been instantly healed."

And his reply? Not, "Well, then, I'm glad you touched me and availed yourself of the power that flows out of me." Not a bit of it. What has healed her? Magic? Verse 48: "Your faith has healed you."

Of course, she's not the only one who learned a huge lesson that day. When this woman confessed her actions in the presence of all the people, what would have struck them is not only what happened to her, but what should have happened to Jesus. She touched Jesus, so her uncleanness should have flowed into him—that should have made him unclean.

Jesus, however, took this understanding of the contagion of uncleanness and used it rather than merely corrected it. He used it to express a truth they may not have gotten otherwise. Instead of the woman's uncleanness flowing into him, he makes it clear that his cleanness is such that it reverses the usual flow of things. His spiritual power is such that it flows backwards into her and drives out the uncleanness and the illness.

Can you see how this relates perfectly to the reverse roofers incident? Which is easier to say: you are ritually clean again or you are healed? Jesus has made the point that an encounter with him accomplishes both, and he's done so by beginning on their terms in order to take them further.

Was he fibbing about feeling the power go out of him and not knowing who touched him? That's coming at it with our questions again, but I'm willing to speculate and be wrong. My guess is that he's so in tune with the Holy Spirit that he can sense power flowing through him from God to people. But I also guess that he knew who touched him and why, that his request for her to identify herself was not so much because he didn't know as because she needed to own her actions and her faith.

The result was that she would have been not only healed of her medical condition but also restored to fellowship in the community as someone made clean and no longer a danger to their purity.

Encountering Jesus can be full of risks as it was for this woman. Blessed are the desperate.

Suggestions for Further Thought

I've talked about an attitude toward God and Scripture that says what we'd never say to a friend: "Never mind about what you want to say to me, here's what I want." Is there some of this in your relationship with God, or is it just me? How do we fix it?

An encounter with Jesus can be an unpleasant experience for us as it was for this woman, full of risks like failure, discovery and the public spotlight. Do you feel those risks? Is it worth it?

Lazarus

Take off the grave clothes and let him go.

John 11:1-53

Now a man named Lazarus was sick. He was from Bethany, the village of Mary and her sister Martha. (This Mary, whose brother Lazarus now lay sick, was the same one who poured perfume on the Lord and wiped his feet with her hair.) So the sisters sent word to Jesus, "Lord, the one you love is sick."

When he heard this, Jesus said, "This sickness will not end in death. No, it is for God's glory so that God's Son may be glorified through it." Now Jesus loved Martha and her sister and Lazarus. So when he heard that Lazarus was sick, he stayed where he was two more days, and then he said to his disciples, "Let us go back to Judea."

"But Rabbi," they said, "a short while ago the Jews there tried to stone you, and yet you are going back?"

Jesus answered, "Are there not twelve hours of daylight? Those who walk in the daytime will not stumble, for they see by this world's light. It is when people walk at night that they stumble, for they have no light."

After he had said this, he went on to tell them, "Our friend Lazarus has fallen asleep; but I am going there to wake him up."

His disciples replied, "Lord, if he sleeps, he will get better." Jesus had been speaking of his death, but his disciples thought he meant natural sleep.

So then he told them plainly, "Lazarus is dead, and for your sake I am glad I was not there, so that you may believe. But let us go to him."

Then Thomas (also known as Didymus) said to the rest of the disciples, "Let us also go, that we may die with him."

On his arrival, Jesus found that Lazarus had already been in the tomb for four days. Now Bethany was less than two miles from Jerusalem, and many Jews had come to Martha and Mary to comfort them in the loss of their brother. When

Martha heard that Jesus was coming, she went out to meet him, but Mary stayed at home.

"Lord," Martha said to Jesus, "if you had been here, my brother would not have died. But I know that even now God will give you whatever you ask."

Jesus said to her, "Your brother will rise again."

Martha answered, "I know he will rise again in the resurrection at the last day."

Jesus said to her, "I am the resurrection and the life. Anyone who believes in me will live, even though they die; and whoever lives by believing in me will never die. Do you believe this?"

"Yes, Lord," she told him, "I believe that you are the Messiah, the Son of God, who was to come into the world."

After she had said this, she went back and called her sister Mary aside. "The Teacher is here," she said, "and is asking for you." When Mary heard this, she got up quickly and went to him. Now Jesus had not yet entered the village, but was still at the place where Martha had met him. When the Jews who had been with Mary in the house, comforting her, noticed how quickly she got up and went out, they followed her, supposing she was going to the tomb to mourn there.

When Mary reached the place where Jesus was and saw him, she fell at his feet and said, "Lord, if you had been here, my brother would not have died."

When Jesus saw her weeping, and the Jews who had come along with her also weeping, he was deeply moved in spirit and troubled. "Where have you laid him?" he asked.

"Come and see, Lord," they replied.

Jesus wept.

Then the Jews said, "See how he loved him!"

But some of them said, "Could not he who opened the eyes of the blind man have kept this man from dying?"

Jesus, once more deeply moved, came to the tomb. It was a cave with a stone laid across the entrance. "Take away the stone," he said.

"But, Lord," said Martha, the sister of the dead man, "by this time there is a bad odor, for he has been there four days."

Then Jesus said, "Did I not tell you that if you believe, you will see the glory of God?"

So they took away the stone. Then Jesus looked up and said, "Father, I thank you that you have heard me. I knew that you always hear me, but I said this for the benefit of the people standing here, that they may believe that you sent me."

When he had said this, Jesus called in a loud voice, "Lazarus, come out!" The dead man came out, his hands and feet wrapped with strips of linen, and a cloth around his face.

Jesus said to them, "Take off the grave clothes and let him go."

Therefore many of the Jews who had come to visit Mary, and had seen what Jesus did, put their faith in him. But some of them went to the Pharisees and told them what Jesus had done. Then the chief priests and the Pharisees called a meeting of the Sanhedrin.

"What are we accomplishing?" they asked. "Here is this man performing many signs. If we let him go on like this, everyone will believe in him, and then the Romans will come and take away both our temple and our nation."

Then one of them, named Caiaphas, who was high priest that year, spoke up, "You know nothing at all! You do not realize that it is better for you that one man die for the people than that the whole nation perish."

He did not say this on his own, but as high priest that year he prophesied that Jesus would die for the Jewish nation, and not only for that nation but also for the scattered children of God, to bring them together and make them one. So from that day on they plotted to take his life.

The first thing to note is that first century folks knew there was a huge difference between people who were sick and those who were dead. The second thing is, as we've mentioned before, Jesus' reputation was that of a healer. So, for instance, Jairus's people come to him and say, "Your daughter is dead . . . Why bother the teacher anymore?" (Mark 5:35; Matt. 9:18 is an abbreviation of this). Similarly, here in the Lazarus story, Jesus' critics say, "Could not he who opened the eyes of the blind man have kept this man from dying?" (John 11:37). They don't ask, "Could he not raise Lazarus?" Keeping someone from death is consistent with Jesus' reputation. Raising someone from the dead is another matter altogether.

And it's not just Jesus' critics. The M sisters are characters whom the author means for us to like, yet they too seem to feel just the same way—Mary in 11:32 and Martha at greater length in 11:21–24. Martha believes in Jesus' power and totally buys that death is not the end of a person. But although they were willing to ask Jesus for help when Laz was ill (11:3), it doesn't seem to cross their minds that they could ask him to raise their brother from the dead. "Our brother is very sick: help him." "Our brother is dead: I wish you could have been here to stop it."

Crowds of people bring the sick for Jesus to heal. We never hear of anyone bringing the recently departed.

Maybe Jesus wanted to avoid any such reputation. Necromancy—doing magic with the dead—was a black art. Maybe this is something Jesus was already accused of. Indeed, the later confusion between Jesus and John the Baptist may be related to necromancy. Jesus can't be the reincarnation of J the B; he's too old. But in the imagination of Herod (Mark 6:14–16) and "the people" (Mark 8:28), he might be magically in league with John's ghost. After all, Jesus had included "the dead raised" in the summary of his ministry in reply to John the Baptist's question "Are you the one?" in Matthew 11:5.

Avoiding the rap of magical concourse with the dead might be part of the reason for Jesus' peculiar public insistence that Jairus's dead daughter was "not dead but asleep" (Luke 8:52). The girl was brought back to life with only a very few witnesses: most of the Twelve had to stay outside; only the inner circle could join the mother and father and Jesus. And even those witnesses were told not to tell anyone about it (though Matthew 9:26 tells us there were big leaks, despite his wishes).

Here too in the Lazarus story Jesus speaks at first about sleeping and waking in verse 11, though he explains to the disciples that he means death.

Another more obvious reason for talking about sleep is to correct the human feeling that death is it. Game over; thanks for playing. Jesus, the Son of God, could be stressing that in the larger perspective—his perspective—true life *begins* when you cash in your chips. Were Jesus to be making this point, it would be very convenient for preachers who have to officiate at funerals. Sometimes we'd love a Jesus who would just waltz into the wake, make light of death and reverse its effects. Paul sings from this song sheet, doesn't he? Pull yourself together—"Where, O death, is your sting?" (1 Cor. 15:55). The brief story of the widow of Nain in Luke 7:11–17 seems to go this route, and the story of Jairus's daughter almost fits.

But it isn't quite that easy with Lazarus. Once again, the gospel writers surprise us by being willing to show Jesus' humanness. In the case of Lazarus, he does not parade in wearing the Kevlar body armour of contempt for mere death. Instead, John's Jesus, who knows and has told people that he will bring Lazarus back from the dead in T minus 6 minutes and counting—this Jesus—weeps (John 11:35).

Why would he do that? Some commentators find this irrational. They look for some other emotion that Jesus could be expressing—say, anger at death's hold on what should be God's world instead of grief at the loss of his friend. But me, I don't find the irrationality difficult. As if emotions were about being rational!

Usually, Christianity drives you crazy with its unintelligible divine paradoxes: one God / three persons . . . how can that be? Well, here's a human paradox in the incarnation, but although we can't understand this one either, we can empathize precisely. Who hasn't felt this emotional contradiction: you can't hurt me / you hurt me very much? To me it's as if Jesus is acknowledging—no, that's too tame a word—it's as if he's experiencing both aspects of death: its desperate sadness from a human perspective but also its limits and impermanence from the perspective of eternity. We go through that all the time. So does Jesus: he's not powerless in the face of death, and his belief in the afterlife is unwavering. Yet he grieves. Death is serious and tragic, especially when the death is that of someone you love. Discussing death in the abstract is one thing. Having an eternal perspective on someone else's grief takes more work. But facing up to the death of your mother or your spouse takes longer and involves more sleepless nights and tissues. We live on a planet where third world populations are dying of hunger and we still get torn up about losing a pet dog or cat. Rationality has nothing to do with grief.

At Lazarus's tomb, Jesus expresses these paradoxical human emotions. No doubt there's an element of truth to the business about anger at death as well as grief—that's true of any mourner. But whatever the emotional mix, Jesus doesn't stop with feelings. He acts upon what he knows. One of the things I miss most about my King James days is the lovely ring of "by this time he stinketh" (John 11:39 KJV) from sister Martha (and it would be fussy Martha who said it, wouldn't it?). Jesus, heedless, rolls away that stone. "Lazarus of Bethany: come on down!" And out pops Lon Chaney Jr., mummy-wrapping trailing behind. O death, where is thy stink?

Rolls away the stone, eh? Hmmm. We're going to hear about that again! The historian in me notes that Lazarus is allowed to stink for four days, whereas

Jesus rose on the third day. There's an obvious parallel between the two stories, but the gospel writer will not falsify the facts in order to make the resemblance of the two stories more striking. Nor does he rein Lazarus's resuscitation into two days in order to make Jesus the new record holder with three.

There's a Lazarus in the famous parable of Jesus in Luke 16:19–31. You remember: *that* Lazarus is a poor man who goes to paradise. Meanwhile, a rich man dies and goes to another place that makes Chinese mustard look tame and wants his tongue cooled. The two Lazarus passages are unique to their separate gospels. The name, which sounds so distinctive to us, is actually the Greek form of a fairly popular Jewish name, Eliezer, which means "my God helps". It's common enough that the two are unlikely to refer to the same person. Still, I get a chill when I read the conclusion to the story in John—that Lazarus's return only makes the Jewish authorities redouble their efforts against Jesus—and compare it with the conclusion to the parable in Luke: "He said to him, 'If they do not listen to Moses and the Prophets, they will not be convinced even if someone rises from the dead'" (16:31).

Suggestions for Further Thought

We're the same way as Mary and Martha, of course, usually very willing to pray for God's healing, never thinking to ask God to raise someone from the dead. Would it be wrong for us to do so?

We know we're citizens of eternity, but we sure feel like children of dust sometimes. We still grieve. Should our grief be different than other people's?

Chasing Out Demons

"Be quiet!" Jesus said sternly.

Luke 4:33–37

In the synagogue there was a man possessed by a demon, an evil spirit. He cried out at the top of his voice, "Go away! What do you want with us, Jesus of Nazareth? Have you come to destroy us? I know who you are—the Holy One of God!"

"Be quiet!" Jesus said sternly. "Come out of him!" Then the demon threw the man down before them all and came out without injuring him.

All the people were amazed and said to each other, "What words these are! With authority and power he gives orders to evil spirits and they come out!" And the news about him spread throughout the surrounding area.

You have to remember that we're dealing with a culture that was somewhat paranoid about sicknesses and death. Almost everyone believed in malevolent beings who were the root cause of many ailments. These critters, though invisible, were nevertheless very real and very dangerous. They were thought to be intent on getting inside of people and doing them ill, often making them ill, in the furtherance of their own nefarious purposes. Prolonged contact with a person, even a friend or family member, who was infested by these creatures meant risking infestation and occupation of your own body. Against these unseen enemies elaborate precautions were sometimes taken, which, of course, sometimes worked and sometimes didn't. When they failed, various experts, with their procedures and unctions, could be called in to effect deliverance and restoration of your body to your own control. Do you think all this is hopelessly naïve and primitive? Well, read it again: every sentence I've written so far is about twenty-first century ideas concerning bacteria. What did you think I was talking about?

No, I'm not saying the first century's ideas about demons were a simplistic way of talking about germs. It'd be convenient if that squared with the text, but it doesn't. What I am saying is that in our own day even people who've never looked through a microscope believe in bacteria and believe they cause diseases. On the face of it, our explanation is every bit as weird and difficult to swallow as belief in demons and that they can cause disease. I can tolerate folks thinking the ancients were wrong, but let's not have any sniffy superiority about how naïve they were to fall for such ridiculous explanations.

It's not like the ancients blamed every disease on the supernatural. They distinguished between the medical and the mystical. "Jesus healed many who had various diseases. He also drove out many demons" (Mark 1:34). "He . . . gave them authority to drive out evil spirits and to heal every disease and sickness" (Matt. 10:1). Not only was there a difference, but it looks as though medical conditions were considerably more common than incidents of demon possession. We have more than twice as many straight healing stories as exorcisms in the gospels. In fact, there are even fewer exorcism stories than stories of nature miracles! Were exorcisms, then, rarer than these lesser known miracles of Jesus?

Do you remember the section about the difference between the miracle stories and the summaries of miraculous healings you find in the background: "Many came to him and he healed them all and cast out their demons." It's true we have more summaries that say nothing of exorcisms. But there are a good number of summaries that do include them, suggesting Jesus dealt with demoniacs more often than the mere handful of occasions we're told about in detail. Many of the summary passages also tell us that people came to Jesus not just with their diseases to be healed but also with demons to be cast out, so Jesus had a reputation as an exorcist as well as a healer of medical ailments.

The exorcism of the man in the synagogue is one of the events that seems to give rise to this reputation. I've got to say I've never understood the demons' tactics in these stories—minions of the supreme evil or not, they seem pretty stupid to me. As soon as they pick Jesus up on visual, they start running off at the mouth. Surely it would be wiser not to call such attention to yourself. "What do you want with us, Jesus of Nazareth? Have you come to destroy us?" Talk about asking for trouble!

What's even worse, they not only start blabbing, but they seem to always tell the truth as well. When did Satan and his underlings come up with this brilliant game plan?

"What do I do if he comes near my victim?"

"Try this: shout loudly about how you don't want him to do anything to you."

"And if he still doesn't leave me alone?"

"Then start telling everyone the truth about him being the Holy One of God and all."

"Yeah, that oughta fix him!"

Yeah, right. The only thing that I can reckon is that they must go into some different mode when they're around him—something sort of in between panic mode and truth-serum mode.

It's odd that Satan himself didn't fall into this self-defeating pattern of behaviour when confronting Jesus at the temptation. Instead, he projected the image of cunning reasonable-sounding manipulator of near-truths we recognize from his snake-in-the-garden days. Are the demons an entirely different and inferior class of act? Or is there something about the business of possessing another being that makes them act this way despite their better judgement? I'd love to know, but not surprisingly, the Bible doesn't seem to have education about the satanic hordes as one of its top priorities.

After telling the loudmouth to be quiet, Jesus does the thing that typifies and distinguishes a gospel exorcism: he speaks, not to the human beings in front of him, but to the demons directly, commanding them to come out. This is otherwise completely out of character for Jesus. In ordinary healings, as we've seen, he is so focused on the healee that he tailors the very method he uses to them. He talks to them: "What would you like me to do for you?" "Be opened!" "Young girl, arise!" In exorcisms, he seems to look right past the person, speaking of the patient in the third person to someone else entirely. "Come out of him!"

The way that the crowd express their amazement should remind you of another story we've looked at. "What is this? . . . He even gives orders to evil spirits and they obey him" (Mark 1:27). Remember the disciples' astonishment at the calming of the storm? "What kind of man is this? Even the winds and the waves obey him!" (Matt. 8:27). The crowds weren't in on that action.

Jesus rebukes evil spirits, he rebukes the wind and the waves, he rebukes fig trees, which represent the spiritual climate and fruitfulness of the nation! He orders dead people to come out of their tombs. What kind of guy is this? A guy who knows how things should be and has the authority to bring that state of affairs about.

So why don't people obey him? I mean, why aren't we compelled to obey him? Why were his followers slow to believe? How could the human authorities be able to openly defy him? Is the human will more powerful than spiritual entities and storms, or was he cutting us some slack he didn't cut demons? Could he have done to the Roman legions what he will do to a legion of demons in our next passage? Could he have ordered the Roman governor— the Roman emperor—to step down? "I command you to come out!" What was he up to?

Suggestions for Further Thought

It's not uncommon to believe that demons were unusually active in the time of Jesus because it was the time of Jesus. And it's probably true that we shouldn't be too quick to see demons as the causes of people's problems. But do demons still possess people today?

It's sometimes thought that a big part of Jesus' ministry on earth was waging war on Satan and his kingdom through the exorcisms. What do you make of this?

Legion

What do you want with me, Jesus, Son of the Most High God?

Mark 5:1–20

They went across the lake to the region of the Gerasenes. When Jesus got out of the boat, a man with an evil spirit came from the tombs to meet him. This man lived in the tombs, and no one could bind him anymore, not even with a chain. For he had often been chained hand and foot, but he tore the chains apart and broke the irons on his feet. No one was strong enough to subdue him. Night and day among the tombs and in the hills he would cry out and cut himself with stones.

When he saw Jesus from a distance, he ran and fell on his knees in front of him. He shouted at the top of his voice, "What do you want with me, Jesus, Son of the Most High God? In God's name don't torture me!"

For Jesus had said to him, "Come out of this man, you evil spirit!"

Then Jesus asked him, "What is your name?"

"My name is Legion," he replied, "for we are many." And he begged Jesus again and again not to send them out of the area.

A large herd of pigs was feeding on the nearby hillside. The demons begged Jesus, "Send us among the pigs; allow us to go into them." He gave them permission, and the evil spirits came out and went into the pigs. The herd, about two thousand in number, rushed down the steep bank into the lake and were drowned.

Those tending the pigs ran off and reported this in the town and countryside, and the people went out to see what had happened. When they came to Jesus, they saw the man who had been possessed by the legion of demons, sitting there, dressed and in his right mind; and they were afraid. Those who had seen it told the people what had happened to the demon-possessed man—and told about the pigs as well. Then the people began to plead with Jesus to leave their region.

As Jesus was getting into the boat, the man who had been demon-possessed begged to go with him. Jesus did not let him, but said, "Go home to your own people and tell them how much the Lord has done for you, and how he has had mercy on you."

So the man went away and began to tell in the Decapolis how much Jesus had done for him. And all the people were amazed.

To us, a guy with an evil spirit is bizarre enough without adding on the extra layers of rough living in the tombs, superhuman strength out of control, the demon (or demons) having the name "Legion" and that whole pig routine. They're not just strange details but perplexing ones. Are we supposed to understand them? Are we allowed to ask about them? What are we supposed to get out of a passage like this?

This is a story full of desperation, violence and avoidance. And these ideas are all mixed together. The townspeople were desperate to avoid the man and chained him up outside of town. The demons were desperate to avoid Jesus' torturing them, begging to be sent into the pigs. The herd of 2,000 pigs rushed away down the steep bank to their deaths. The man begged Jesus to take him with him while the townspeople pleaded with Jesus to leave. Everyone is violently rushing and frantically begging for something to go away or to be allowed to go away. All this blur and clamour going on all around Jesus. And somehow, he's in the middle of it all, calm and in control.

In a Jewish context, this story also reeks of uncleanness. You start out in Gentile country, not a very promising beginning. Plus you've got a guy who lives among the unclean dead. He's troubled by unclean spirits. These eventually flee into unclean animals. Ugh. Just add anchovies for a completely disgusting scenario.

Given the Roman name "Legion" and the nonkosher livestock, commentators understandably wonder if there is some symbolic meaning here. Lots of folks at the time probably thought that priority one for a messiah of Israel should be to remove the Romans who were possessing their land and send the unclean swine back where they belong. Or is this perhaps a statement about satanic forces possessing the pagan Romans? While the overall mood of this passage seems to support a political interpretation, when it comes down to the actual workings of the story, there's no deciphering scheme that works convincingly.

What gets me is not what it might have abstractly symbolized but what it must have been like in real life. Look again at verses 1–6 and imagine yourself in the disciples' sandals round about verse 6. There's this crazy, violent wild man. You see him in the tombs off in the haze. And as you spot him in the distance, you notice that he also spots you. He seems to look straight through you. He tilts his head and then . . . How do you feel as he breaks into a run, charging straight at you and Jesus? Are your feet still in those sandals? Are they wet?

But these demons, powerful as they are compared with human beings, cannot threaten Jesus or even negotiate in terms of their own powers. I don't mean they can't scare him; I mean they literally can't even threaten him. Not only are they compelled to tell the truth about Jesus and his relationship to God, they fall down before him and implore him not to torment them. And they do so "by God"—by Jesus' Father—not the demons' own master! Again, odd behaviour in demons!

This is the one exorcism in which Jesus asks the name of the demon(s) he encountered. Other religions and magical systems regarded the names of things as significant ways of gaining power over them, and this passage is sometimes thought to lend credence to the occult practice of seeking the name of demons in order to use them or defeat them. But in Mark 5 it is almost certainly due to the singular/plural nature of the possession rather than some kind of technique Jesus employed in order to gain the upper hand on some evenly matched opponent. Even the demon(s) recognize that Jesus holds all the cards well before there's any talk about names. Indeed, Jesus' command to "come out" doesn't appear to have made use of the name (the events are narrated out of sequence in 5:7–9).

There's some confusion over whether there is one demon named "Legion" or a legion of demons whose individual names we don't know. The Greek of the possessed man's reply goes back and forth between singular and plural. Jesus has asked, "What is your (singular) name?" and the reply is "My (singular) name is Legion for we (plural) are many." The legions of the Roman army were of course well known at that time and not a pleasant thought. It comes as a surprise when we're told there were about 2,000 pigs, though, since the lowest number you'd expect in a legion would be double that, and probably more like triple. Are we meant to think that there were 2,000 demons in there—and a pig for each one? I doubt it. This whole singular/plural muddle probably has more to do with our lack of understanding of spirits than anything else.

Knowing as little about demons as we do, it remains unclear why they should want to go into a herd of pigs. I'm biased, I know, but I'm inclined to think that they'd prefer people to pigs—perhaps they knew there was no point in asking Jesus if they could go into some other person. I guess to a demon, pigs are better than nothing for some reason, and there was a reasonable chance that the Jewish Jesus would feel less protective of unclean pigs than, say, a herd of cute fluffy sheep.

Nor, sadly, do we get much further looking at the kamikaze pork routine. It's worth saying the man tried to hurt himself while possessed as well. He seems to have avoided rushing down the steep banks but did try to cut himself (Mark 5:5). If he was suicidal, though, he was remarkably unsuccessful for such a strong bloke. It's difficult to see how destruction of a host could further a demon's purposes, but it was said that the demon in the boy in Mark 9 often threw him into fire or water to kill him. That's the father's take on the events, at least. It's possible that in both cases what looked like self-harm was an attempt of the human to get at the spirit.

So, again, should we be asking about these details—trying to make sense of them? I think so. But with people like us, from a culture that has tried its hardest for years not to believe in, much less understand, spiritual realities, nobody should be surprised if we can't quite put it all together. We're allowed to look and ask, but we've also got to be willing to stop and refocus on the main idea. The gospel authors treat the realities of the spirit world in the same way they treat the workings of the natural world. They don't intend to teach you how or why demons flit between hosts any more than they intend to teach you how and why cold fronts cause storms on the Sea of Galilee. What they intend to do is tell you about this remarkable rabbi's mastery over both. The main emphasis of the story is Jesus, his radical new cleanness, his power to restore people to the way they were meant to be and the polarized reaction that his work causes. Compared to those themes, particular stuff about demons and pigs are interesting distractions.

And Jesus *is* the master here, in the midst of all this desperation and begging and fleeing and crashing. If I were filming this, I'd use that special effect where the main character is walking tall in slow motion, while around him all the traffic and pedestrians are rushing, blurred in time lapse. Yet only this slow-motion Jesus knows what he's doing and does it.

Suggestions for Further Thought

Most people today don't believe in demons but might respond more warmly if you changed the story so it was about mental illness. What features of the story make that tempting? Do you think it's right or wrong to paraphrase it that way?

Spend some time praying to the God who is superior to any other force or being. Thank him for his love and protection.

Unless You People See Miracles . . .

"Unless you people see signs and wonders," Jesus told him, "you will never believe."

John 4:46–54

Once more he visited Cana in Galilee, where he had turned the water into wine. And there was a certain royal official whose son lay sick at Capernaum. When this man heard that Jesus had arrived in Galilee from Judea, he went to him and begged him to come and heal his son, who was close to death.

"Unless you people see signs and wonders," Jesus told him, "you will never believe."

The royal official said, "Sir, come down before my child dies."

"Go," Jesus replied, "your son will live." The man took Jesus at his word and departed. While he was still on the way, his servants met him with the news that his boy was living. When he inquired as to the time when his son got better, they said to him, "Yesterday, at one in the afternoon, the fever left him."

Then the father realized that this was the exact time at which Jesus had said to him, "Your son will live." So he and his whole household believed.

This was the second sign Jesus performed after coming from Judea to Galilee.

Jesus was doing some earth-changing things. He fed thousands, showing that God can and will provide for ongoing needs. He showed his power and ability to triumph over Chaos and external dangers like storms. He demonstrated his capacity to take care of internal physical or spiritual problems through the healings and exorcisms. I'm sure you'd agree that this is great and important stuff. Is this why he came?

I hope it isn't. I'm not saying this to be critical, but you or I wouldn't be satisfied with these "solutions". If we were tackling the problem of safety on the high seas, we'd be happier using any mastery over the winds and waves to alter and stabilize the climate in such a way as to avoid destructive storms in the first place. Or at least provide a reliable warning system. The appearance of a rainbow before a destructive storm would serve us better than having it appear afterward.

If the goal is to feed the hungry masses, why not provide everyone with a basket that multiplied bread and fish, like Elijah's friend who got a jar that never ran out of oil? Failing that, he could have provided more efficient farming techniques or cross-bred high-yield crops. A one-off provision of pita and sardines hardly seems an answer to the problem of hunger.

And why didn't Mr. Heal-from-a-Distance just heal everyone from a distance? I've made out like it was really cool that he dealt with individuals rather than diseases, but there's something to be said for the other method. Isn't the elimination of smallpox a greater accomplishment than the curing of one or ten or a thousand cases? Instead of curing a blind man or three, why not use the occasion to pronounce all blindness a thing of the past? Why not get tough on all fevers and the cause of fevers?

Well, here's why not. Miracles are a significant part of Jesus' work on earth; they are characteristic of his ministry. But miracles, even the healings that seem to have been so common, were not central to his ministry. He said in Luke 13:32–33, "I will keep on driving out demons and healing people today and tomorrow, and on the third day I will reach my goal . . . No prophet can die outside Jerusalem!" He did not come to this planet in order to cure diseases and heal people. In fact, he didn't heal everyone. His father, Joseph, almost certainly died before Jesus did and was not raised from the dead. Jesus was able to restore the ear of the temple guard that had been cut off, but he did not restore the head of John the Baptist. The healing of the paralytic in John 5 seems to have taken place in the presence of other people waiting for help, but the ensuing story implies that only he was healed. The man whom Peter and John healed in Acts 3 is said to have been afflicted since birth and begged at the temple gate every day. He was about forty years old. Jesus, who would have been in the vicinity more than a few times, didn't heal him. I think I could almost get away with saying the healings were a "side effect" of his real mission, but that's probably pushing it. Better to say that they were a peripheral part of it, pointing in to the center.

In all four gospels, the miracles have something to do with faith. Sometimes they're a response to faith, but they're always a stimulus to provoke faith or stimulate a growth in faith. The author of the fourth gospel loves to call them "signs", pointing to something greater than themselves. They are microcosmic examples of who Jesus is, pointing to a larger picture of him.

Yet Jesus seems unhappy using these mighty works to "prove" himself and cause faith to grow where there is none. We often say the miracles are about provoking faith, but it's more involved than that. They're not designed to provoke faith directly. They're certainly not about giving in to demands. In Mark 8:11–12, he refused to provide a miraculous sign to some who sought proof. And in the story of the royal official here in John 4, you can't help reading verse 48 in a somewhat disappointed voice, "'Unless you people see signs and wonders,' Jesus told him, 'you will never believe.'" And as an attempt to provoke faith, they don't always work. Even the raising of Lazarus in John 11 couldn't force Jesus' opponents to change their minds. And John says later, "Even after Jesus had done so many miraculous signs in their presence, they still would not believe in him" (12:37).

In this story, in fact, the healing performed at a distance constitutes a test of faith. The man went to Jesus in order to beg him to come to the sick son's bedside (4:47). He has no intention of leaving until this Healer agrees to come with him and heal his son. But Jesus won't go. Instead, he tells the man to go home on his own, with just Jesus' word about healing. Imagine leaving your dead car on the side of the road, trudging a couple of miles to the garage and asking the guy to come down the road to look at it. The mechanic looks you in the eye and says, "You can go back on your own. Your car will work now." What do you say? "Okay, great; thanks." Tip your hat and back you go? The guy in John 4 does and only gets partway back before he's picked up (4:50–51).

Say rather that the miracles are about Jesus showing who and what he is, and the identification of himself with his Father. It is that opportunity to glimpse who and what he is that should provoke and encourage the embers of faith. He doesn't do the miracles in a calculating spin-doctory photo-op way. Instead, he often responds to people out of compassion. His compassion reveals as much about him as his ability to respond with a miracle.

But Jesus made some extravagant promises about his followers. "All who have faith in me will do the works I have been doing, and they will do even greater things than these" (John 14:12). Or how about, "If you have faith and do not doubt, not only can you do what was done to the fig tree, but also you can say to this mountain, 'Go, throw yourself into the sea,' and it will be done. If you believe, you will receive whatever you ask for in prayer" (Matt. 21:21–22).

From time to time in the history of the church, people have tried to take these statements to mean simply what they appear to say: that God will do virtually anything a believer or two in agreement want. That'd be the natural way to understand these promises, except we know Jesus' teaching is rarely straightforward. There have been times in those 2,000 years of warfare and injustice and martyrdom when literal and figurative mountains were ripe for sudden jaunts to the seaside. Has there never existed anyone with adequate faith? Or is it possible that Jesus meant something different by "greater things" and has a different standard for doing the impossible?

The Bible itself acknowledges the problem even if it doesn't provide a catchall answer. One has only to think of Paul and his "thorn in the flesh", probably some illness preventing him from getting on with his work. He prayed for it to be removed. And when it didn't happen, he prayed again—prayed not once, not twice but on three occasions and to no avail (2 Cor. 12:7–9). Later in this book, we'll see Jesus himself act just this way.

One of my colleagues, Max Turner, has argued that when Jesus says, "Whatever you ask in my name", what he means is like those old cop shows, "Open up in the name of the law!" You're not allowed to say that if what you mean is "This is what I want and I hope it is consistent with the law." You're only allowed to say it when acting as an agent of the law and in the process of enforcing it. We sometimes invoke the name of Jesus to bless our own requests, but neither Jesus nor the law works quite that way.

So the Christians of Acts, for instance, still did healings, but Acts holds nothing rivalling Jesus' miracles as such. The "greater things" they do include converting Jews by the thousands and bringing the good news to the very heart of the Roman Empire. As Clare, one of my students, reminded me, if it's harder to get a rich man to enter the kingdom of God than to push a camel through the eye of a needle, then some of the apostles and some of your friends (and maybe you) have done a "greater thing" already.

Suggestions for Further Thought

Could God ever use you to perform a miracle?

Does prayer sometimes work and sometimes not? Or is that the wrong question?

Spiritual and
Radical

Relationship with the Father

The Son can do nothing by himself; he can do only what he sees his Father doing, because whatever the Father does the Son also does. For the Father loves the Son and shows him all he does.

John 5:16-47

So, because Jesus was doing these things on the Sabbath, the Jewish leaders began to persecute him. In his defence Jesus said to them, "My Father is always at his work to this very day, and I too am working." For this reason they tried all the more to kill him; not only was he breaking the Sabbath, but he was even calling God his own Father, making himself equal with God.

Jesus gave them this answer: "Very truly I tell you, the Son can do nothing by himself; he can do only what he sees his Father doing, because whatever the Father does the Son also does. For the Father loves the Son and shows him all he does. Yes, and he will show him even greater works than these, so that you will be amazed. For just as the Father raises the dead and gives them life, even so the Son gives life to whom he is pleased to give it. Moreover, the Father judges no one, but has entrusted all judgment to the Son, that all may honor the Son just as they honor the Father. Whoever does not honor the Son does not honor the Father, who sent him.

"Very truly I tell you, whoever hears my word and believes him who sent me has eternal life and will not be judged but has crossed over from death to life. Very truly I tell you, a time is coming and has now come when the dead will hear the voice of the Son of God and those who hear will live. For as the Father has life in himself, so he has granted the Son also to have life in himself. And he has given him authority to judge because he is the Son of Man.

"Do not be amazed at this, for a time is coming when all who are in their graves will hear his voice and come out—those who have done what is good will rise to live, and those who have done what is evil will rise to be condemned. By myself I can do nothing; I judge only as I hear, and my judgment is just, for I seek not to please myself but him who sent me.

"If I testify about myself, my testimony is not true. There is another who testifies in my favor, and I know that his testimony about me is true.

"You have sent to John and he has testified to the truth. Not that I accept human testimony; but I mention it that you may be saved. John was a lamp that burned and gave light, and you chose for a time to enjoy his light.

"I have testimony weightier than that of John. For the works that the Father has given me to finish—the very works that I am doing—testify that the Father has sent me. And the Father who sent me has himself testified concerning me. You have never heard his voice nor seen his form, nor does his word dwell in you, for you do not believe the one he sent. You study the Scriptures diligently because you think that in them you possess eternal life. These are the very Scriptures that testify about me, yet you refuse to come to me to have life.

"I do not accept glory from human beings, but I know you. I know that you do not have the love of God in your hearts. I have come in my Father's name, and you do not accept me; but if someone else comes in his own name, you will accept him. How can you believe since you accept glory from one another but do not seek the glory that comes from the only God?

"But do not think I will accuse you before the Father. Your accuser is Moses, on whom your hopes are set. If you believed Moses, you would believe me, for he wrote about me. But since you do not believe what he wrote, how are you going to believe what I say?"

Jesus is our example of what it means to be spiritual. He's also an example of what it means to be radical. This goes deeper than the miracles he performed. If he didn't come in order to heal and feed people, perhaps he came in order to become a radical and spiritual model for us to emulate. That's what we'll look at throughout this section.

Some people love it when Jesus talks as he does in our reading above. John evidently did; he records more of these passages about "I and the Father are one" and "may they be in me as I'm in you" than the other three gospels put together. I have to confess, however, that I often find them tough going. "On that day you will realize that I am in my Father, and you are in me, and I am in you" (John 14:20). I need to steel myself to tackle them with about the same resolve as tackling twisted-up telephone cords.

When you get the words untangled, they're always about some facet of the close connection between Jesus and his Father, a theme close to John's heart. Even apart from the identification of Word and God the author of the gospel tells us about in the first chapter, Jesus himself has already spoken in 4:34 about doing the will and work of the one who sent him. This sentiment will be repeated in more personal and intimate terms later in the book (for instance, John 10:14–17; 14:10–11, 31; 15:9–11). And again in passages such as John 10:30 he himself asserts that he and his Father are one.

Although John's gospel is most insistent about these ideas, they are not absent from the other gospels. In Mark 14:36, Jesus uses the Aramaic term *Abba*. Scholars are almost universally agreed that the Swedish commercial pop band is not quite ancient enough to be in view here; instead, this familiar form of "father" shows a direct and intimate relationship with God.

Back at Jesus' baptism in Mark 1, also told in Matthew 3 and Luke 3, a voice comes from the sky: "You are my Son, whom I love; with you I am well pleased" (1:11). But Jesus probably has a sense of this even earlier. Luke relates the story of the boy Jesus inadvertently left behind in Jerusalem during a family trip there. His parents return to find him making himself at home in the temple, and when they say they've been looking all over, he replies, "Didn't you know I had to be in my Father's house?" (Luke 2:49). Even though Luke has only just asserted the virgin birth in the previous chapter, I doubt Jesus intends this to be a teenager's stinging rebuke to Joseph—he goes with them easily enough with no indication he'd rather stay here in his "real" father's house.

In fact, despite all this close self-identification with the Father, Jesus never belittles other people's potential for relationship with God. His message is not "I'm closer to him than you'll ever be." It is true no one has seen the Father but the Son, and to disconnect from Jesus is to hang up on the Father. Even so,

Jesus seems to constantly invite or assume an intimate Father-offspring relationship for others as well as himself. He teaches his disciples to address God with a similar level of intimacy, for instance, in the Lord's Prayer, "Our Father" (Matt. 6:9). Quite probably *abba* lies behind the Greek. There is a paradox here: he is uniquely the Son yet calls for us to become as close to the Father as he is (John 16:26–27; 17:20–26). Later, Galatians 4:6 and Romans 8:15 demonstrate that the word *abba* became used for all believers' relationship to the Father, even in churches that wouldn't have spoken Aramaic.

Here in John 5, the business starts with Jesus having healed the ungrateful paralytic on the Sabbath day when work was supposed to be off the menu. Jesus told them the Father was working and it was right for him to be working as well. Our familiarity with the passage and with who John thinks Jesus is blinds us to the potential offensiveness of Jesus' argument. We only hear Jesus saying his usual stuff in which he identifies his work, mission and method with God's. We hear him saying, "You know God never stops; here is another instance."

This isn't how the Jewish authorities heard it. They come to the conversation with a much clearer picture of the transcendence of God. On high, he has made rules for us mortals to follow in our little lives on earth. My guess is Jesus' argument sounded to them like the child who, discovered doing something out of bounds, gets just that tone in her voice as she says, "Well, *you* do it, Dad! Why can't I?"

It's perhaps not only that the Jews objected to the intimacy of Jesus being Son, but that they objected to the presumptions Jesus made on the basis of sonship. The way Jesus seemed to claim such a peculiar relationship with God seemed to make him equal to God rather than a loved subject—as though the God-given scriptural rules did not apply to him. *God is allowed to work on the Sabbath, and so can I, his Son.* By putting himself above the rules like that, was he thinking of a sonship that involved superseding the Father's authority? Wasn't he acting in a way that implied God would have to move over and make room for him?

Such an understanding of the Jewish authorities' objections helps us understand the logic of the speech Jesus gives in reply. The first half is an attempt to explain what we've assumed but his opponents have not. Jesus is not a separate son claiming his own equal right to make or break rules. Jesus is not wrestling and wresting some kind of authority away from an uncooperative God the Father. On the contrary, it's all about the Father teaching the Son what to do, showing him how to act and giving him authority to give life to the dead (as he has already demonstrated by raising the official's son in John 4 and will again in the Lazarus story in John 11).

Moreover, God has entrusted the Son with authority to judge. If the Son's authority is given by the Father, Jesus shows no disrespect by doing God-only stuff. Rather, it is the authorities who diss God by not honoring the work God does through the Son whom he authorized to do it. Verse 30 summarizes the thrust of this first half of the speech.

That represents Jesus' self-defense about his relationship with the Father. The second half of the speech begins in verses 31 and 32, which say, "Don't take my word for it; here are other places to look for confirmation." The first is the testimony of John the Baptist about Jesus (esp. John 1:15, 29, 32–34). The second is the nature of the works Jesus is doing. The authorities have filed Jesus' actions under "V" for "Violations, Sabbath". Jesus suggests they should think again. These are not instances of rule breaking that happen to involve healings or other good works. They are instances of good works that sometimes entail setting aside the rules. The more concerned you are about the letter of the law, the more likely you are to see a pattern of violations. The more concerned you are with what God wants to do for people and the world, the more likely you are to see Jesus' life as showing a very different pattern— God's own pattern.

The final witness are the Scriptures that set out the very rules Jesus is accused of breaking. He goes out of his way to focus on Moses. And here the defense has barbs as Jesus goes on the offensive. He hammers home from the Scriptures they diligently study the implications of what he said earlier (5:23) about the honor being due to the Son as well as to the Father.

The authorities were correct. Jesus' spirituality and his radical nature are built on the same foundation: his close and unique relationship with the Father. He sees his whole identity as tied up not in himself but with his Father, God (5:30). But this is not the same as having no self-worth. To assert, as he has, that Moses wrote about him and that he deserves to garner the same sort of honor due to God is making a huge claim indeed.

Suggestions for Further Thought

Should we call God "Abba"? Isn't it true that Jesus' relationship with God is much closer than our own?

Can you blame the Jewish authorities? How would you feel about someone who came to you and said, "If everyone doesn't honor me, they are all dishonoring God"?

Prayer: Public and Private

Lord, teach us to pray.

Luke 11:1–13

One day Jesus was praying in a certain place. When he finished, one of his disciples said to him, "Lord, teach us to pray, just as John taught his disciples."

He said to them, "When you pray, say:

> " 'Father,
> hallowed be your name,
> your kingdom come.
> Give us each day our daily bread.
> Forgive us our sins,
> for we also forgive everyone who sins against us.
> And lead us not into temptation.' "

Then Jesus said to them, "Suppose you have a friend, and you go to him at midnight and say, 'Friend, lend me three loaves of bread; a friend of mine on a journey has come to me, and I have nothing to set before him.' And suppose the one inside answers, 'Don't bother me. The door is already locked, and my children and I are in bed. I can't get up and give you anything.' I tell you, even though he will not get up and give you the bread because of friendship, yet because of your shameless audacity he will surely get up and give you as much as you need.

"So I say to you: Ask and it will be given to you; seek and you will find; knock and the door will be opened to you. For everyone who asks receives; those who seek find; and to those who knock, the door will be opened.

"Which of you fathers, if your son asks for a fish, will give him a snake instead? Or if he asks for an egg, will give him a scorpion? If you then, though you are evil, know how to give good gifts to your children, how much more will your Father in heaven give the Holy Spirit to those who ask him!"

Jesus' life seems full of private prayer. His usual pattern is to go to lonely places and pray on his own, sometimes for marathon sessions. "Very early in the morning, while it was still dark, Jesus got up, left the house, and went off to a solitary place, where he prayed" (Mark 1:35). "Jesus went out to a mountainside to pray, and spent the night praying to God" (Luke 6:12). The gospel writers tell us particularly about his prayer sessions before (Luke 9:28) and after (Matt. 14:23) big events. But let's face it, anywhere you open a gospel, if you're not right before or after a big event, it's because you're in one! Even when Jesus wants some company on the eve of his arrest, he takes some of the guys along to pray but pulls away from them anyway (Matt. 26:36–40).

But there's the public element as well. Jesus prays with people around more often than I'd realized. For example, when raising Lazarus from the dead in John 11, his prayer is public and self-consciously so. It's aimed at his Father all right, but it's meant to have effects on the people who hear it as well: "Father, I thank you that you have heard me. I knew that you always hear me, but I said this for the benefit of the people standing here" (John 11:41–42).

A few chapters on, John 17 is amazing. Jesus prays for himself, for his disciples and then for you and me: "My prayer is not for [these disciples] alone. I pray also for those who will believe in me through their message" (John 17:20).

Or how about chapter 10 of Luke? At the return of the seventy-two disciples, he spontaneously combusts into prayer in front of them. This is Jesus as we rarely see him. "Jesus, full of joy through the Holy Spirit" (Luke 10:21). A happy Jesus! The outburst has earned the nickname "the bolt from the johannine blue" because Jesus here sounds so unlike his usual manner in Matthew, Mark or Luke.

In our passage, Luke 11, Jesus is off praying some place, typically. Verse 1 makes it sound like the guys are waiting quietly at a respectful distance until he's finished. Then one of them asks, "Teach us to pray, just as John [the Baptist] taught his disciples." As it happens, none of the gospel writers really tell us anything about John's prayer life. We do know from Luke 5:33 that John's disciples had a reputation for prayer and fasting.

Luke's version appears to leave off the ending and very beginning. Matthew's (6:9–13) starts "Our Father" instead of just "Father". This is almost certainly a translation thing. Both gospels were composed in Greek and Jesus probably prayed this in Aramaic. As we said last time, the word *abba* probably lies behind both.

Beginning a prayer this way seems unremarkable to us, but contrast it with the typical Jewish opening: "Blessed are you, O Lord our God, King of the universe." We see Jesus himself using a variation on this, but including "Father" in Luke 10:21: "I praise you, Father, Lord of heaven and earth." The personal and relational "Father" is balanced by "Lord of heaven and earth".

Even in the Lord's Prayer, the intimacy of the appeal to God as *Abba* is tempered by the clauses that follow. "Hallowed be your name, your kingdom come" are both acknowledgments that even though God is personal and personally involved, he is still holy Lord and King, not merely my good ol' cosmic buddy. Both Judaism and Christianity hold this tension between God's involvement and his transcendence. It's such a tightrope walk that you're constantly trying to redress the balance by leaning to one side or the other. To the person who conceives of God only as cold, distant Creator, you need to stress the intimacy—he's there with you all the time—but to the person who thinks of God as their own personal girlfriend/boyfriend, you need to go another direction entirely. Jesus' sense of balance is exemplary.

Despite the modern tendency to reduce all talk of God's kingdom to talk of God's kingship or rule, the phrase "your kingdom come" is not voicing the desire for God to begin being king, as if his coronation is coming up real soon now. Rather, it is the wish there will soon be a kingdom that responds properly to his kingship—a community or a people who live as fellow subjects under the king.

The prayer then moves from the lofty to the day-to-day: the bread we need for the day. This will have reminded the disciples of the wilderness following the exodus, in which God provided a daily supply of manna for each family to gather rather than a monthly tabernacle freezer chest of bulk-buy pita.

I love the way this prayer takes unexpected turns like this. Here's another: "Forgive us our sins, for we also forgive everyone who sins against us," reminiscent of Jesus' parable of the unmerciful servant in Matthew 18:23–35.

I also love the honesty of "Lead us not into temptation" rather than "Give me strength to withstand trials". Jesus teaches us to pray from the heart. The spirituality of Jesus is never about the appearance of holiness. As we'll see when we talk about Gethsemane, he himself prayed to avoid his trial. But this prayer is the starting point in the process of communication with God rather than the end point. Praying is supposed to do something to you as well as to the Person you're asking.

The parable that follows, the friend at midnight (11:5–8), is another outrageous passage if you really read it. Look how immediate it is: "Suppose you have a friend, and you go to him . . ." You, of course, are the pray-er in this story, and the friend inside represents God, to whom you're praying. What is Jesus' picture of God? He says, "The one inside answers, 'Don't bother me'" (11:7). In so many of his parables Jesus flirts dangerously with irreverence. The God character says, "Don't bother me." Jesus will have angered some of his hearers, as with the later parable of the unjust judge (again a scandalous portrayal of God, Luke 18:1–8).

The next segment—"Which of you fathers . . . ?"—helps. Reading this, you get the sense that the parable was not presenting you with a comprehensive picture of God any more than this is presenting a picture of his hearers' parenting skills. The argument in both cases is from the lesser to the greater: if even an unfriendly friend will respond to this kind of entreaty, then how much more will a friendly one? And if earthly fathers know how to give, how much more will the heavenly one?

Jesus' prayer life is marked by balance, honesty, boldness and persistence. It's clear that prayer is based upon that close relationship with and respect for God, but it's also clear there's nothing wrong with praying for personal needs. That's where prayer starts out, anyway.

Suggestions for Further Thought

Luke's version of the opening suggests that Jesus is giving his disciples words to say rather than just a pattern to follow: "When you pray, say . . ." (Luke 11:2). How do you feel about reciting prayers as opposed to spontaneous prayers?

Does the Lord's Prayer teach us to ask for the big things or to be honest and realistic?

Keeping the Law: A Jewish Spirituality

Whoever practices and teaches these commands will be called great in the kingdom of heaven.

Matthew 5:17–24

"Do not think that I have come to abolish the Law or the Prophets; I have not come to abolish them but to fulfill them. Truly I tell you, until heaven and earth disappear, not the smallest letter, not the least stroke of a pen, will by any means disappear from the Law until everything is accomplished. Anyone who sets aside one of the least of these commands and teaches others accordingly will be called least in the kingdom of heaven, but whoever practices and teaches these commands will be called great in the kingdom of heaven. For I tell you that unless your righteousness surpasses that of the Pharisees and the teachers of the law, you will certainly not enter the kingdom of heaven.

"You have heard that it was said to the people long ago, 'You shall not murder, and anyone who murders will be subject to judgment.' But I tell you that anyone who is angry with a brother or sister will be subject to judgment. Again, anyone who says to a brother or sister, 'Raca,' is answerable to the Sanhedrin. And anyone who says, 'You fool!' will be in danger of the fire of hell.

"Therefore, if you are offering your gift at the altar and there remember that your brother or sister has something against you, leave your gift there in front of the altar. First go and be reconciled to that person; then come and offer your gift.

esus was neither a Protestant nor a Catholic. His spirituality, rooted in his close relationship with his Father and expressed through his prayer life, is at heart a Jewish spirituality. It's understandable we so often have trouble remembering that. He and his followers had frequent disagreements with the way Judaism was practiced in their day. Those will come more clearly into focus in our next encounter. But it's important to recognize they were internal criticisms. The major players—Jesus, Peter, James, even Paul—were as Jewish as chicken soup and matzos. If the New Testament emphasizes the differences, it is not because Judaism is so wrong it needs constant hammering but because the two theologies are so close that the differences become very significant.

Most people know that the Christian church split off from Judaism. At least that's the easiest way to think of it. But at least some of the biblical authors saw it the other way round. Old Testament Judaism prepared God's people for Jesus, and at Pentecost and the gate called Beautiful, thousands and thousands of Jews became convinced of Jesus' messiahship. Did they split off from Judaism, or did what we call Judaism now split off from the ongoing work of the God who inspired all the prophecies?

Jesus' teaching is not far from Jewish instruction of the day—he's brilliant, but not without precedent. They too used parables, they too summarized the Law, they too exhorted people to live in a way consistent with God's love for them, they too thought of God as Father. The various phrases in the Lord's Prayer we've just looked at all have parallels in the Talmud, even if no other rabbi put them together in just that way.

I've written about the way Jesus prayed in public as well as in private. It's easy to miss the fact that part of his public praying would have been done in the synagogues. "On the Sabbath day he went into the synagogue, as was his custom" (Luke 4:16). His Jewish practice was such a part of his life (and that of the disciples) they barely mention it—we tend to hear about it only when Jesus teaches or heals in the synagogues. Even so, if you've got a concordance or a computer Bible, do a quick search through the gospels for all the mentions of *synagogue* or *synagogues* and you'll find quite a handful, most of them about Jesus going there.

Of his trips to the temple, we tend to remember only the dramatic showdown with the dove sellers and money changers. But he spent a lot more time in the temple doing ordinary things, apparently. He doesn't seem to attempt to disrupt the sacrifices themselves, and he sits without objection and observes money being collected for the temple funds (Mark 12:41–44), even when they accept an impoverished person's last few coins. He seems to be comfortable with synagogue and temple.

Just after our passage in Matthew 5, Jesus exhorts his hearers not to make oaths by heaven or by earth or by Jerusalem, "For it is the city of the Great King" (5:35). And within the passage, the person offering a sacrifice at the altar is told to be reconciled *before* he makes his sacrifice, not *instead* of making his sacrifice, although there would be good Old Testament precedent for that as well: "I desire mercy, not sacrifice" (Hosea 6:6 NIV). Jesus' saying here is less radical about temple worship than were the Old Testament prophets! (He does use this verse on other occasions, however: Matt. 9:13; 12:7.)

From occasional comments in the gospels, we also know he and his disciples were aware of the regular Jewish festivals, and because of the importance of the Lord's Supper, we particularly hear about his preparations and celebration of the Passover, the most important of the Jewish holidays. There are hints the celebration matches the traditional Seder liturgy very well, right down to closing by singing the "Hallel" psalms (Ps. 113–118; Mark 14:26, "When they had sung a hymn, they went out"). More about this special Passover meal later.

John 10:22–23 places Jesus in the temple in Jerusalem for the festival celebrating the temple's restoration and rededication. Somewhere in between Malachi and Matthew, Israel fell into the hands of foreigners, and a group known as the Maccabees rose up out of nowhere to defeat a world-class superpower and take back Jerusalem and the temple. What an appropriate time and place to ask Jesus to clarify whether or not he is the Messiah (who will rise up out of nowhere to defeat a world-class superpower). For the moment, however, the main thing to notice is that Jesus has come for this national celebration (you may know it as Hanukkah).

We frequently think the main problem with the Pharisees was they had too many laws. Jesus himself, though, says he has not come to do away with the Law or the Prophets, and the problem with the Pharisees and others is they don't live up to what they know (Matt. 5:20; 23:2–3).

It is overwhelmingly probable Jesus even kept to the Jewish food laws. I know he taught in such a way that finally undermined them. But look at the way all modern translations of Mark 7:19 have the critical phrase "In saying this, Jesus declared all foods clean" bracketed out as an aside. Know why? Because of Acts 10. Most people reckon Peter is responsible for most of the stories in Mark. But in Acts 10:12–16, where Peter has a vision of nonkosher foods and cries out, "I have never eaten anything impure or unclean" (v. 14), it's clear that Peter, eight chapters after Pentecost, is still keeping a strictly kosher table. Our best guess is he only realized Jesus was speaking about all foods being clean much later, when retelling the story, and he or Mark probably smacked his forehead with the heel of his hand: "That's what that was all about! He was saying that even back then." But this means Peter didn't realize it then . . . And that means Jesus' teaching and example could not have been unambiguously against the kosher laws. Unless Jesus also kept to the kosher food laws throughout his life, there's no way Peter would have made such vehement and orthodox objections in Acts 10.

Jesus transformed and fulfilled Judaism. He didn't set it aside. He did everything he did within Judaism, even if he sometimes seemed to be undermining and bending it to breaking. But that's the subject of our next passage.

Suggestions for Further Thought

Why would Jesus undermine the food laws but then keep to kosher law himself?

If Jesus was so Jewish, why shouldn't we become Jewish?

Flouting the Law

The Son of Man is Lord even of the Sabbath.

Mark 2:23–3:6

One Sabbath Jesus was going through the grain fields, and as his disciples walked along, they began to pick some heads of grain. The Pharisees said to him, "Look, why are they doing what is unlawful on the Sabbath?"

He answered, "Have you never read what David did when he and his companions were hungry and in need? In the days of Abiathar the high priest, he entered the house of God and ate the consecrated bread, which is lawful only for priests to eat. And he also gave some to his companions."

Then he said to them, "The Sabbath was made for people, not people for the Sabbath. So the Son of Man is Lord even of the Sabbath.". . .

Another time Jesus went into the synagogue, and a man with a shriveled hand was there. Some of them were looking for a reason to accuse Jesus, so they watched him closely to see if he would heal him on the Sabbath. Jesus said to the man with the shriveled hand, "Stand up in front of everyone."

Then Jesus asked them, "Which is lawful on the Sabbath: to do good or to do evil, to save life or to kill?" But they remained silent.

He looked around at them in anger and, deeply distressed at their stubborn hearts, said to the man, "Stretch out your hand." He stretched it out, and his hand was completely restored. Then the Pharisees went out and began to plot with the Herodians how they might kill Jesus.

t seems Jesus kept the kosher food laws even while he undermined their necessity. The same is probably also true of the sacrificial system. It didn't take long for the first Christians to realize Jesus' own sacrifice made animal sacrifices inappropriate (Heb. 10:10). And yet, if Jesus had not gone through with the usual Jewish routines of sacrifices, we surely would have heard about it and the authorities would have made something of it. Instead, they find remarkably little to complain about.

But there are a few areas where Jesus seems to always be on the edge of breaking the law. One is the whole "uncleanness" business. There are lots of Old Testament regulations about what you may and may not touch. Certain kinds of diseases make you unclean, and anyone who touches you is automatically also unclean. You'll remember the story of the woman who snuck up and ambushed the hem of Jesus' garment—his cleanness spread to her rather than the other way around (Luke 8:44).

Touching dead people or animals will also do it to you. Jesus seems to conform to this idea when he tells some of his opponents they're like whitewashed tombs, looking nice on the outside but filled with unclean things (Matt. 23:27). We've looked at the Lazarus passage, in which Jesus stands at a safe distance, but there are other revivals from death where Jesus goes right in there. When the mourners stop their procession in the story of the widow of Nain, it's because Jesus has touched the coffin (Luke 7:14). And worse than that, when he raised Jairus's daughter from the dead, he took her by the hand (Mark 5:41). This episode leads to a peculiar sort of question: if he's brought a dead girl back to life, has he touched a clean or unclean person?

The disciples also are accused of eating with ceremonially yucky hands, not because they've touched a dead or sick person but because they haven't gone through the ritual wash (Mark 7:2–4). But this has an easy answer. Unlike the prohibitions relating to sick or dead folks, the traditions about methods of hand washing are rooted in good Jewish tradition rather than in Scripture (Mark 7:8). Jesus' spirituality obviously made a distinction between the demands of Judaism he regarded as traditional and those he regarded as from the Scriptures.

Within the gospels, however, the most frequent source of friction between Jesus and Jewish practice revolved around the Sabbath, in particular, Jesus' apparent willingness to do things that were regarded as "work" on the Sabbath.

The most frequent events are the healings—in reading through the gospels, you sometimes wonder if Jesus ever healed anybody on a weekday! The Old Testament is very clear about the importance of not doing work on the Sabbath—punishable by death sometimes (Num. 15:32–36)—but less clear about where to draw the line between "work" and just hanging around.

Jewish tradition allowed a bit of latitude. Temple-related work was generally exempt (Num. 28:9; 1 Chron. 23:31). If someone's life depended on it, you could even fight (see 1 Macc. 2:40–41 in the Apocrypha). It's not always possible to locate Jesus' defense of his own practice specifically in any of the exemptions, but they're clearly in line. A typical response is that it's right to do good on the Sabbath, to pull sheep out of a pit (Matt. 12:11–12).

Jesus is on weaker ground, however, in this incident about the disciples out in the field picking grain. At least they're not poaching. Jewish farmers were required to permit passers-by to pick some of the crop; they had to leave some of their crop specifically for that purpose (Lev. 19:9–10)!

Their crime wasn't gleaning without a license, but gleaning in a nongleaning zone: namely the Sabbath. Harvesting was one of those things specifically outlawed by Scripture (Exod. 34:21), so Jesus doesn't defend them on the basis that their opponents are again hung up on the "traditions of men".

I suppose you could base a defense on the definition of "work". Reaching out and picking a bit of grain as you happen to be walking past is not the same thing as revving up the scythe and spending the day filling up the old barn. Jesus doesn't go this way either, though. Nor does he try to make out that the boys were famished and close to death. So what was his explanation?

Typically, Jesus tells them a story—a curious one from 1 Samuel 21:1–6. David and his men eat some forbidden bread, just as Jesus' people wind up picking and eating this forbidden grain. Within Judaism, the holiness of a place is not dissimilar to the holiness of a set-apart time, so the parallel is more apt than it might appear.

Jewish literature tells us this passage troubled later rabbis. David was the chosen one of God, so his violation of the law here must have been in some way justifiable. Jesus was obviously exploiting this same feeling. By applying it to himself, he made it not an exercise in understanding David but a means for a unearthing deeper questions about who Jesus is and the place of the law within spiritual life.

Here's an answer you'll often hear: Jesus can do what he likes on the Sabbath because, as God, he is Lord of the Sabbath (and everything else). But this is too simplistic. The point of the Davidic parallel cannot be "Jesus is Lord over the Sabbath just as David was Lord over the Tabernacle". How do we get from the story to the conclusion Jesus draws?

The answer comes from what looks almost like a mistake in Mark's text. In verse 26 Jesus says, "In the days of Abiathar the high priest. . . ." Abiathar will have been there at the time, but he's not mentioned until the next chapter, and his father is high priest at this time. Some say the reference is an error by Jesus, others say it's Mark's error, some point at the Old Testament itself. Still others point out there is no real error involved at all if the passage is translated "in the days of Abiathar the high priest" rather than the unnecessarily limiting "when Abiathar was high priest".

But why refer to a guy who's not involved in the story? Perhaps it's for the same reason as an American might say "in President Lincoln's day" in preference to "when James Buchanan was president". Most settle for this kind of reasoning. Abiathar was by far the more famous of the two.

We only get somewhere when we ask *why* he was famous. First, when the time came, Abiathar aligned himself with God's new chosen king, David, rather than Saul (1 Sam. 22:20–21; 23:6). The second thing is very similar. Along with Zadok, Abiathar oversaw the transference of the Ark of the Covenant to Jerusalem (2 Sam. 15:29), again aligning himself with a new way of doing things.

What characterized "the era of Abiathar the high priest"? God-given changes in the rules that governed how the Jewish nation was to worship and know their God. It's no mistake that this passage follows the saying about new wine requiring fresh wineskins (Mark 2:22).

Here's what should have chilled spines when Jesus referred to this story: Jesus' opponents, had they been alive in the days of Abiathar, would have aligned themselves against David's pantry raid. They would have stoned the great king before he ever took the throne, just as they were plotting to kill Jesus in this present time of change.

The law was never meant to be the solid thing upon which the love between God and humanity must be based. Jesus' spirituality recognizes the rules were made to nurture the relationship, not the other way round. You see this same mistake in the divorce controversy: the regulations were added not because God wanted divorces but as a damage control response to human failings (Mark 10:2–5).

God's rules matter. Jesus stayed within the spirit of the law by following its trajectory, its intent. And he condemned the lawyers of his day, who managed to do wrong while staying within the letter of the law by finding and exploiting what they thought were loopholes in wording (see, for instance, the Corbanite Maneuver, Mark 7:9–12, or the replacement of "banned" words with synonyms, Matt. 5:22). How typical of Jesus to leave his listeners to work out the devastating implications of his claim to be the Lord of the Sabbath in a time of change, an era of Abiathar.

Suggestions for Further Thought

What do you understand the Jewish Sabbath to be? Is there any value in it for Christians?

Is it true that rules can nurture relationship, or are the two always opposed?

Suppers with Sinners

Why does your teacher eat with tax collectors and sinners?

Matthew 9:9–13

As Jesus went on from there, he saw a man named Matthew sitting at the tax collector's booth. "Follow me," he told him, and Matthew got up and followed him. While Jesus was having dinner at Matthew's house, many tax collectors and sinners came and ate with him and his disciples. When the Pharisees saw this, they asked his disciples, "Why does your teacher eat with tax collectors and sinners?"

On hearing this, Jesus said, "It is not the healthy who need a doctor, but the sick. But go and learn what this means: 'I desire mercy, not sacrifice.' For I have not come to call the righteous, but sinners."

In many brands of religious devotion, you find little shrines in nooks of the home—lots of shiny bits draped around images or statues and flowers and maybe some candles. Judaism hadn't messed around with that kind of stuff since Josiah got rid of the household gods (2 Kings 23:24). There was an altar at the tabernacle or temple, there was a Torah shrine of sorts at the synagogue. There was a religious focus to home life, but it wasn't off in the corner. Jewish home religious life happens around whatever passes for the dining room table. The Sabbath meals, the Passover Seder, this is where it all takes place: an altar with a tablecloth. It's no surprise then that for orthodox Jews even today, much of the concerns of ritual purity revolve around the kitchen and the table: candles, kosher meals, tithes of food and even of the spices used in the foods.

For a first century Jew, having dinner with someone was making a statement about acceptance and about religious fellowship. Supper was not just sustenance; supper was spirituality. Doing lunch was doing theology.

And Jesus was a guy who would chow down with just about anybody. He accepted dinner invitations from upstanding Pharisees (Luke 7:36; 11:37; 14:1), but he also swapped snacks with less savoury souls. Having a reputation for eating with tax collectors and sinners was not unlike being a known associate of politicians and gangsters.

You won't find this facet of his life covered in much depth in the meal stories. Rather, as with miraculous healings, there are summaries and other statements about his practice. In Luke 15:2 the religious authorities muttered, "This man welcomes sinners and eats with them." In Matthew 11:18–19 and its parallel in Luke 7:33–34, we find an odd sort of saying about how John the Baptist and Jesus just couldn't win with their opponents. John fasted and was a teetotaller and didn't please them, whereas Jesus ate and drank and they called him a glutton and drunkard, a friend of tax collectors and sinners. The historian in me notes there is no way any skeptic can think the gospel writers or early church would have made up such a saying; the accusations must have their roots in Jesus' historical opponents, which in turn means no one can deny this characteristic of Jesus.

Short-stuff Zacchaeus, up in the tree, was a tax collector to whom Jesus said, "Ahoy the tree, aren't you going to invite me over?" (See Luke 19:5.) There's the surprise of acknowledging his presence, the presumption of Jesus inviting himself not merely to dinner but to stay overnight and a shock of sudden acceptance that entailed. "You mean me? You're willing to be my guest? Whoa! I mean, yes, certainly."

Matthew, also called Levi, was another tax collector with whom Jesus took tea. Jesus said to Matthew what he'd said to at least some of the other disciples, "Follow me!" and like the guys who left their nets, Matthew left his "booth" and followed him (as Luke explicitly states in 5:28). I wonder if Jesus told him he would become a "tax collector of men" the way Peter and Co. were told they'd catch people (Matt. 4:19).

Tax collectors were lumped in there as collaborators with the Romans. In most other client states of the empire, the people would have been taxed by their own government until the time of Roman occupation when the taxes get diverted to Rome. In Israel, however, the temple tax continued to be due as well as the Roman taxes, so it was seen as an added burden rather than a displaced duty. But as well as being regarded as Roman puppets, even among the Romans like Livy and Cicero, tax collectors garnered a reputation for collecting more than they should have. It was so widespread in Palestine that even a guy who lived in the desert and ate bugs knew about it: when John the Baptist preached about the coming judgement, tax gatherers in his audience asked what they should do. John's reply shows he knew about their usual practices: "Don't collect any more than you are required" (Luke 3:13). Even Jesus used them as an example of self-serving when he said, "If you [only] love those who love you, what reward will you get? Are not even the tax collectors doing that?" (Matt. 5:46)

The tax situation was complicated then as it is now. Essentially, there were direct taxes like income tax and land tax and indirect taxes like import/export duties and road-use taxes. The word used to describe Matthew and the fact he had himself a little booth meant he belonged to the bureaucracy that collected the indirect ones. The rabbinic literature is pretty scathing about both types, but Matthew's type comes off worse. Imagine owing money to a foreign country as well as the taxes you already pay, and imagine that money being collected by a guy with the attitude of a government tax man and the financial motivations of a used-car salesman and you'll get the aroma of "His friends are tax collectors and sinners".

So there's the holy man, Jesus, at Matthew's house, having a dinner party with tax collectors and sinners. That's just great: if you're trying to start a new movement, these are precisely the people you wouldn't want your photo taken with.

Although it could be used more generally of any non-Pharisee, the word *sinners* here implies people with a lifestyle that put them on the wrong side of the Old Testament law: criminals, prostitutes and so on. Again, Jesus seems to have constantly had this attitude of giving respect to the unrespectable.

It's sometimes thought the Pharisees regarded such people as beneath them and beneath God's notice. This isn't really fair. They collided with Jesus on this matter because it was shared ground; their goals were so different but so similar. The Sadducees, in contrast, don't quarrel much with Jesus about the "sinners"; all they really care about is religious orthodoxy in the abstract and what gets done in the temple. From their perspective, Jesus can hang around with whoever he wants on his own time. But the Pharisees, like Jesus, are interested in the restoration of people who are far from God. So they too would rejoice over a tax collector who truly left his evil ways behind and began a new relationship with God. For the Pharisee, however, it was important to do it that way round. The initiative in these things belongs with God. God offered covenant, a pattern for living with him. It is up to people to accept his yoke. And acceptance of that yoke shows acceptance of and life inside that pattern.

To the Pharisees, it must have looked as though Jesus was offering "cheap covenant", as if he were saying, "Never mind what God wants you to do, he accepts you even if you do evil." Jesus' way was to bring people to their responsibility by showing God's love; the Pharisees' way was by living in God's love and announcing it to others in the hope they'd accept the responsibilities and thereby find themselves experiencing it as well. Very close; very far apart. They well understood Jesus' reply to them about the physician being around those who are ill. But they would have wanted to see him preaching to "sinners" as a superior rather than drinking with them as if a partner in crime.

Suggestions for Further Thought

Jesus presented a paradigm of openness and acceptance toward tax collectors and "sinners", having fellowship with them before they changed their evil ways. How can our churches be more like this?

Even so, Jesus turned away potential followers who wouldn't give away all their money (Mark 10:21) or who insisted on putting family obligations first (Matt. 8:22). When should we model his love and acceptance, and when is it right to "shake the dust from our feet" (Mark 6:11)?

Criticism for Authorities

Teacher, when you say these things, you insult us also.

Luke 11:37-54

When Jesus had finished speaking, a Pharisee invited him to eat with him; so he went in and reclined at the table. But the Pharisee was surprised when he noticed that Jesus did not first wash before the meal.

Then the Lord said to him, "Now then, you Pharisees clean the outside of the cup and dish, but inside you are full of greed and wickedness. You foolish people! Did not the one who made the outside make the inside also? But now as for what is inside you—be generous to the poor, and everything will be clean for you.

"Woe to you Pharisees, because you give God a tenth of your mint, rue and all other kinds of garden herbs, but you neglect justice and the love of God. You should have practiced the latter without leaving the former undone.

"Woe to you Pharisees, because you love the most important seats in the synagogues and respectful greetings in the marketplaces.

"Woe to you, because you are like unmarked graves, which people walk over without knowing it."

One of the experts in the law answered him, "Teacher, when you say these things, you insult us also."

Jesus replied, "And you experts in the law, woe to you, because you load people down with burdens they can hardly carry, and you yourselves will not lift one finger to help them.

"Woe to you, because you build tombs for the prophets, and it was your ancestors who killed them. So you testify that you approve of what your ancestors did; they killed the prophets, and you build their tombs. Because of this, God in his wisdom said, 'I will send them prophets and apostles, some of whom they will kill and others they will persecute.' Therefore this generation will be held responsible for the blood of all the prophets that has been shed since the beginning of the world, from the blood of Abel to the blood of Zechariah, who was killed between the altar and the sanctuary. Yes, I tell you, this generation will be held responsible for it all.

"Woe to you experts in the law, because you have taken away the key to knowledge. You yourselves have not entered, and you have hindered those who were entering."

When Jesus went outside, the Pharisees and the teachers of the law began to oppose him fiercely and to besiege him with questions, waiting to catch him in something he might say.

A s we said, Jesus didn't only eat with tax collectors and sinners—he also shared that sign of acceptance and fellowship with the Pharisees and authorities, which is a turn of events you might not have expected. In this passage, Luke implies there's a link between Jesus' speaking and the invitation. We don't stress it often, but this wouldn't be the only time Jesus' teaching had a positive impact on the religious authorities. In Mark 12:28, a Pharisee starts up a conversation with Jesus precisely because he has given a good answer to someone about the resurrection.

The Pharisees were not always the bad guys. Some of them, at least, had some notion that Jesus was up to the same sort of thing they were. They invited Jesus to supper; they would not have invited a total heretic or an evil monster. On another occasion, in Luke 13:31–32, far from trying to kill him, some of them came to Jesus to warn him Herod was after him and the net was closing.

They invited Jesus and he accepted the invitation. But these dinner parties always left a bad taste in the Pharisees' mouths. And you can't help feeling their invitations weren't entirely friendly. This is perhaps especially true of the first supper in Luke 7:36–50. Jesus was invited, but apparently his host didn't provide any of the normal tokens of welcome. In that culture, as in many others, the duty of the guest was to act overly grateful for whatever the host offered, and Jesus did not complain. Not at first. But when the "sinful woman" came and anointed his feet to the disgust of the host, Jesus dropped all social pleasantries and drew public attention to the woman's actions, comparing this sinner favorably to his host's lack of hospitality!

There's another Pharisee clambake after our passage, in Luke 14:1–24. At that one, it's not just the host who came in for a rough ride but all the guests as well. They're all told off for seeking the best seats—for their self-importance and self-promotion.

Our passage in Luke 11 falls right between the two and features Jesus coming to the tea party and insulting just about everyone in sight. And this time there's little indication they've done anything wrong. It cannot be that they did not provide Jesus with anything to wash his hands, because the Pharisee is surprised Jesus has not. The word used for "surprised" generally means something positive, although it can be as strong as "outraged". The Pharisee tsk-tsking self-righteously would be enough to set Jesus off, I suppose.

It seems to me this is a different incident from the one recorded in Mark 7 and Matthew 15 in which some Pharisees expressed disapproval when the disciples didn't do their ritual hand washing. Less clear is whether this is the same rant we find in Matthew 23. It certainly contains some of the same complaints about the authorities, the "woe to you's" or, as Eugene Peterson has rendered them, "You're hopeless!" But these are just the sort of sentiments that do get repeated on different occasions, whenever the person feels the injustice. Jesus criticized the authorities regularly, sometimes in a backhanded sort of way: "Unless your righteousness surpasses that of the Pharisees and the teachers of the law . . ." (Matt. 5:20) but often with a directness and vehemence that must have been shocking to all who witnessed it, as in this passage.

It's worth noticing Jesus meant what he said about following the Pharisees' talk but not their walk (Matt. 23:2–3). Even at his most vehement, he was not criticizing their Judaism, not even criticizing the oral law, the traditions of the fathers per se. Rather, he criticized particular people for their attitude toward and practice of these things. He had no problem with tithing spices; his beef was with those who tithed the mustard but kept the hot dogs all to themselves. Even the bit about "loving the best seats" was not an argument for total equality in the synagogue, much less the dissolution of the synagogue in favor of meeting in the marketplace. There will always be more important seats at a banquet or synagogue; what Jesus hates is the attitude of seeking those places, of trying to project and enhance your own importance.

The "unmarked graves" saying (Luke 11:44) reminds us of the more explicit saying in Matthew 23:27: "You are like whitewashed tombs, which look beautiful on the outside but on the inside are full of the bones of the dead and everything unclean."

The section that follows on the "experts in the law" is frightening to those of us in academia. These experts were Pharisees too; it isn't that some people were Pharisees and the experts were of another party. It's more likely those called Pharisees were the practitioners and the experts were the scholars. They expected Jesus to feel differently about them the same way evangelical scholars go to great lengths to separate themselves from, say, TV evangelists. The experts were people with the deepest respect for the Scriptures; they were obsessed with studying the minutiae. In our day, they'd be the folks doing and supervising the doctorates.

If the scholars expected Jesus to apologize for implying something negative about them, they were sadly mistaken. They loaded other people down with burdens without doing anything practical to help, they did historical research into acts for which they should have been repenting and they obscured the keys to knowledge, not only failing to enter into relationship with God themselves but hindering other people from doing so. This is a very painful passage for those of us who write commentaries.

Making yourself important either by ostentatiously doing religion or by doing scholarship about religious topics is not what this Jesus values. Come as a little child. There's no point in standing up straight on the stage behind the podium. Climb a tree; that's about the only way you'll get Jesus to look up to you. This Jesus is the kind of guy who lifts shorty Zacchaeus by saying, "I must stay at your house," but insults the living daylights out of the self-important who chime, "Oh, but darling, you absolutely must dine at our house."

Suggestions for Further Thought

Is there any room for religious authorities and experts within Christianity, or should they all just get "real jobs"?

Jesus rebukes the religious for tithing even their herbs but neglecting the larger picture. We all know who are the Pharisees of today, right? Anyone who is more fundamentalist than we are. Resist that temptation to judge others for a moment. What are your own particular narrow foci, and what larger picture do you struggle to keep in view?

Busting Up the Temple

He overturned the tables of the money changers.

Mark 11:15-19

On reaching Jerusalem, Jesus entered the temple courts and began driving out those who were buying and selling there. He overturned the tables of the money changers and the benches of those selling doves, and would not allow anyone to carry merchandise through the temple courts. And as he taught them, he said, "Is it not written: 'My house will be called a house of prayer for all nations'? But you have made it 'a den of robbers.'"

The chief priests and the teachers of the law heard this and began looking for a way to kill him, for they feared him, because the whole crowd was amazed at his teaching.

When evening came, Jesus and his disciples went out of the city.

In my business, New Testament studies, it's no longer fashionable to call this story the cleansing of the temple. Some interpretations of the life and message of Jesus require him to judge a temple of which he disapproved rather than cleanse a temple he regarded as holy. Call it what you will, the meaning seems plain enough from what is and is not contained in the biblical account.

As we saw in the previous encounter, Jesus didn't hold back for the sake of politeness or appearance. He doesn't mess around here either. No, he does not lodge a strongly worded complaint or picket the money changers' tables or hand out leaflets discouraging the purchase of doves. Instead, he's an extremist, a one-man Greenpeace. He drives out the merchants. In the story in John 2:15, he drives them out with a whip as if they themselves were the animals! And he overturns the tables of the money changers. Can you picture it—coins scattering everywhere—slow-mo panning shot—Matrix-like bullet time?

This must have been quite a scene. But what was its purpose? Against whom was it directed? Look at the text—the primary target was those who were buying and selling, the money changers, those selling doves and finally anyone carrying merchandise through the temple courts.

Who were the money changers and dove sellers, and why were they in the temple? These are two very different sets of people. For some reason, you weren't allowed to use ordinary coins in the temple but had to change over to an approved set of coins. This would make sense if we were talking about stuff like Disney Dollars or turnstile tokens minted by the temple itself, especially since Jews were so obsessive about avoiding images. Ordinary coins, as we know from the "give to Caesar" passage, often had images on them. What's baffling, though, is that the coins used by the temple were also foreign and had even more offensive images on them. So why this money had to be used we don't really know. Tradition or convenience, I guess.

The dove sellers are another story entirely. They're not mere tradition; instead, we're talking about people who provided sacrificial animals for a system that was still heavily into animal sacrifice as a way of showing respect and love for God. And this isn't exactly their fault; it's what he authorized in the Old Testament Scriptures. Lots of people no longer kept livestock, of course. The life of a Jerusalem city dweller living three blocks from the temple was very different from that of a nomadic herder tooling around the wilderness behind the tabernacle. These guys provided a way for worshipers to express themselves through animals by sacrificing some cash.

Up until the years around Jesus' visit, the sacrifice sellers weren't allowed to peddle inside the temple at all, but did their dove dealing out on the Mount of Olives. Moving this trade inside was more than a little controversial: "It wasn't like that in my day!"

Was this recent move indicative of a secularization and commercialization of the temple? Has this degenerated to the point where businesspeople were using this part of the temple as just another section of the city, suitable for business traffic? Only Mark's version adds the explicit reference to people carrying "merchandise through the temple courts" (Mark 11:16).

What were these temple courts? Where does this all happen? In the very center, the Holy of Holies? No, Jesus would not ordinarily have been allowed even to approach the heart of the temple, and we have no record of him trying. In the inside Court of the Priests, where the temple hierarchy did their business? No. In the Court of the Levites or the Court of the Men, where ordinary worshipers would have been separated from the "real business" of worship, which only the priests could perform—was this an attack against that? No. Was it even in the outer Court of the Women? Nope. We're talking about the outer-outer area of the temple grounds: the Court of the Gentiles, where anyone could go.

This is not about worship; this is not even about the corruption of the temple hierarchy of priests. The priests react, to be sure, but they come in for no direct criticism in any of the four gospels. Instead, it all revolves around merchandise. In John's story, Jesus explicitly says, "Stop turning my Father's house into a market!" (2:16). Using the temple to make money should have been just as offensive as working on the Sabbath day. That's not what it's there for.

The Christians who wrote the gospels, of course, were doing so at a time when their spirituality and that of Israel were parting company. You can be assured if Jesus had, at this or any other point, come out strongly against the temple, they'd have found it relevant enough to remember and record. Similarly, as we'll see in the next section, Jesus' enemies had strong motivation to present him to the Roman governor as being guilty of some kind of temple-related offence. What was blasphemy to a Jew seemed totally innocuous and unintelligible to a Roman, but Rome had temples of its own and took temple violation very seriously. Once again, if Jesus had attacked the temple rather than tried to cleanse it, his opponents wouldn't have had to resort to the false witnesses whose testimony couldn't be collaborated.

It is the stories that come before and after the temple cleansing that hint at judgement. We've already looked at the cursing of the fig tree; some see the fig tree as symbolic of Jesus' judgement on the literal institution of the temple and the literal city of Jerusalem. It seems much more likely the leafiness of the tree and the commercial success of the temple outer courts are both symbolic.

This is again an attack not on Jewish religion itself but on the superficiality and hypocrisy Jesus finds among some of its practitioners.

Jesus quotes Jeremiah 7, the prophet's outrage about the people's falseness in religion and abuse of the temple. Here is another unstated hint at judgement—this chapter of Jeremiah goes on to threaten the destruction of the temple. Commentators sometimes overlook, however, that the very same chapter also contains the verse "Reform your ways and your actions, and I will let you live in this place" (v. 3 NIV). Neither Jesus' action nor the chapter in Jeremiah is primarily about the judgement and destruction of the temple itself, but rather about the falseness of the people's practice and how seriously God takes it.

In Luke, the temple cleansing is preceded by Jesus looking out over Jerusalem and speaking about the coming destruction he foresees. But Jesus is weeping about that destruction (Luke 19:41) as he will wrestle emotionally with his own fate in the garden of Gethsemane shortly (Luke 22:44). Luke has arranged thus for a saying about the temple's destruction to immediately precede the account of the temple cleansing (Luke 19:44–45). Then as now, some people misunderstood this as Jesus threatening the temple, but the gospel writers go out of their way to stress that any such threat was a misunderstanding (John 2:19–21). How ironic that some New Testament scholars regard themselves as having proved something that the Sanhedrin, on the spot, could not (Mark 14:57–59).

And yet it is true that Jesus, through his own sacrifice and death, did undermine the practices of the temple. Never mind the dividing line between priest and worshiper, the very curtain separating off God's inner sanctum was torn in half (Mark 15:38)! But he accomplished it through his death rather than it being part of his teaching.

The earliest Christians only came to understand it slowly, while continuing to attend the temple (Acts 3:1) and even going through purification rites that included sacrifices there (Acts 21:23–26). The Christians had probably already come to understand that these things were not necessary for God's salvation, but unnecessary did not automatically mean eliminated or undesirable.

Judaism was not some failed experiment Jesus and the Christians tried to replace. Pretend the temple is the House of Representatives or Parliament. Jesus isn't here denouncing the Speaker or the representatives. He's throwing out the lobbyists representing commercial interests. The spirituality of Jesus and the early Christians involved outspoken action against human hypocrisy but not against institutional religion as such. Then as now, Jesus was more interested in the stance of the people's hearts than the structures in which they gathered for worship.

Suggestions for Further Thought

Is Christianity something different than Judaism, or is it a continuation? Does it bring about an end or a completion; does it abolish or reaffirm?

When I go round to a church or other groups to share about Jesus, my publisher wants me to take a stack of my books with me to sell. Would this be okay with Jesus, or would he overturn the book table?

A Humble Chutzpah

So he got up from the meal . . . and began to wash his disciples' feet.

John 13:3-15

Jesus knew that the Father had put all things under his power, and that he had come from God and was returning to God; so he got up from the meal, took off his outer clothing, and wrapped a towel around his waist. After that, he poured water into a basin and began to wash his disciples' feet, drying them with the towel that was wrapped around him.

He came to Simon Peter, who said to him, "Lord, are you going to wash my feet?"

Jesus replied, "You do not realize now what I am doing, but later you will understand."

"No," said Peter, "you shall never wash my feet."

Jesus answered, "Unless I wash you, you have no part with me."

"Then, Lord," Simon Peter replied, "not just my feet but my hands and my head as well!"

Jesus answered, "Those who have had a bath need only to wash their feet; their whole body is clean. And you are clean, though not every one of you." For he knew who was going to betray him, and that was why he said not every one was clean.

When he had finished washing their feet, he put on his clothes and returned to his place. "Do you understand what I have done for you?" he asked them. "You call me 'Teacher' and 'Lord,' and rightly so, for that is what I am. Now that I, your Lord and Teacher, have washed your feet, you also should wash one another's feet. I have set you an example that you should do as I have done for you.

T his is crazy. Where is the logic in that long sentence making up verses 3 and 4? Jesus knew all things were under his power so he got up and washed the disciples' feet?! There's a paradox running through all of the gospels, and we see it clearly here. On the one hand, he's as humble as can be. "What do you want me to do for you?" is his main question (Mark 10:36, 51). He miraculously makes bread for others to eat but regards making bread for himself as a temptation. In a culture that regards feet as a dirty part of the body, Jesus gets down on the floor and washes his disciples' feet. This was a job usually reserved for Gentile slaves, whose dress Jesus emulated by taking off his outer clothes and putting the towel around his waist.

If you met such a guy, you'd tell him he has serious self-esteem problems. You'd expect those actions to go with an attitude of "Oh, don't worry about me" and "I'm useless at this stuff; you guys go ahead." But Jesus isn't like that.

Because on the other hand, Jesus has a very high opinion of himself: he is self-confident to the point where, if anyone else acted this way, we'd call him arrogant and conceited. Jesus thinks more than the world of himself. He believes how you feel about him will determine how God will feel about you on the last day (Luke 9:26; John 3:18). Jesus deliberately commanded people to follow him. Seriously, what would you think of someone who came to visit with a dozen other guys following him? "Who are these guys?" "Oh, these are my disciples." Great.

He's like this all through the gospels. In one chapter, he claims to have come not in order to be served but to serve (Matt. 20:28 or Mark 10:45) but then in the next chapter, he accepts the adulation of the crowds—the hosannas and palm branches (Matt. 21:9 or Mark 11:9). He not only accepts it but, according to Luke 19:39–40, refuses the requests to calm his fan club down. The requests were probably made not only because of the impropriety of the scene but because of the danger of the Romans misconstruing the gesture as the beginning of a revolt. No, Jesus not only accepts it but answers it has to be this way; if not these people, the very stones would cry out.

And even dressed in his slave outfit, Jesus tells his disciples, "You call me 'Teacher' and 'Lord', and rightly so, for that is what I am" (John 13:13). And then he tells them what to do! What a guy! Is this chutzpah or humility?

You've got to love Peter here. When he gets it wrong, he gets it spectacularly wrong; you know he means well and does occasionally get it spectacularly right. All the disciples must have been extremely uncomfortable with this whole scenario, but the way John tells it, none of them says anything. John even makes it sound as though Jesus actually washed others before coming to Simon Peter (vv. 5–6). When he comes to Peter, though, the poor fellow can't contain himself. Make sure you read this question with the emphases on the right words: "Lord, are *you* going to wash *my* feet?" (v. 6). According to Matthew, John the Baptist had the same sort of problem at Jesus' baptism, although then the water was on the other foot (as it were): "I need to be baptized by you, and do you come to me?" (Matt. 3:14).

This could easily turn into a comedic scene, with Peter whipping on a towel of his own and the two of them dancing around each other, each trying to splash water on the other's feet while keeping their own dry. "I'll wash you!" "No, I'll wash you!" Peter almost starts down this road in verse 8: "No, you shall never wash my feet." But Jesus' reply in verse 8 is somewhat surprising and stark; it amounts to, "You let me wash you, or we're through."

See? He's done it again. Just when you think he's at his humblest, he goes and says something like that. Is he humble or is he high-handed?

I doubt Peter understood the resonance here that the gospel writer does— either you let Jesus cleanse you, or you're finished. But Peter's answer could not have been better. He says, "Then, Lord . . . not just my feet but my hands and my head as well!" (v. 9) Typical Petrine flip—one second he's "No way", and the next, "Go for it". But here he does the U-turn not because he gets the theology exactly but because he reads Jesus. That's a great starting point for any disciple, and Jesus' rejoinder concerning the disciples being those who've had baths (except for one of them) is probably about their following him.

Putting his normal clothes back on, Jesus tells them they should wash each other's feet. He has set an example for them to do what he has done.

Know what, though? It doesn't happen. At least we're never told about it. The feet of the twelve disciples get into the act very specifically in the book of Acts, where there seems to be a ritual involving people selling land and placing the proceeds at the feet of the apostles (Acts 4:35–5:2), but we're never told about these guys washing anyone else's feet through the whole New Testament. Well, not literally, anyway. They do in other ways, however, such as when Peter argues Paul's case alongside him in Acts 15, or when Paul argues for Peter's rights in 1 Corinthians 9:5 (cf. Peter's priority in Acts 15:5–8).

There are other differences as well. We are to take Jesus' example and serve each other. But I'm not sure we're called to talk to people the way he did: "You stand there and take it, or you and I are finished." There are aspects of Jesus' spirituality and attitude that we must never emulate, such as receiving the praise and even worship of a set of disciples. There are others that we must take great care in emulating, such as his criticism of authorities to the point of causing disruptions in places of worship! But we are called to follow his example in such matters as his close relationship with the Father and his attitude of serving. We are not exactly what he is, we cannot do precisely the things he did, but we are to have the same mind, the same attitude of self-giving, whoever we are and whatever we do.

Suggestions for Further Thought

Can you think of other examples in which Jesus was both humble and certain of his own importance at the same time?

Are there times when it's right for us to be humble and firm at the same time? Is there someone who acted this way with you and perhaps you thought they were being hypocritical?

Crucified and
Resurrected

Did He Have To Die?

This shall never happen to you!

Matthew 16:15-25

"But what about you?" he asked. "Who do you say I am?"

Simon Peter answered, "You are the Messiah, the Son of the living God."

Jesus replied, "Blessed are you, Simon son of Jonah, for this was not revealed to you by flesh and blood, but by my Father in heaven. And I tell you that you are Peter, and on this rock I will build my church, and the gates of death will not overcome it. I will give you the keys of the kingdom of heaven; whatever you bind on earth will be bound in heaven, and whatever you loose on earth will be loosed in heaven." Then he ordered his disciples not to tell anyone that he was the Messiah.

From that time on Jesus began to explain to his disciples that he must go to Jerusalem and suffer many things at the hands of the elders, the chief priests and the teachers of the law, and that he must be killed and on the third day be raised to life.

Peter took him aside and began to rebuke him. "Never, Lord!" he said. "This shall never happen to you!"

Jesus turned and said to Peter, "Get behind me, Satan! You are a stumbling block to me; you do not have in mind the concerns of God, but merely human concerns."

Then Jesus said to his disciples, "Whoever wants to be my disciple must deny themselves and take up their cross and follow me. For whoever wants to save their life will lose it, but whoever loses their life for me will find it.

ouldn't he have avoided the whole thing? As far as we can tell, he spent almost all of his time in the villages among the ordinary people, and very little time in the big cities like Jerusalem. And he was right to avoid them; everyone knew the cities were dangerous for someone like Jesus. Once when Jesus proposed going to Jerusalem to see Lazarus when he was ill, the disciple Thomas (whose name in the original Aramaic means literally "the one [who is] like Eeyore") remarked sarcastically, "Oh good, let's all go so we can all be killed" (John 11:16, translation mine). It seems like Jesus could have just avoided Jerusalem and probably lived to a ripe old age.

Even having decided to put himself in danger, the Jesus of the gospels doesn't have any trouble getting out of difficult situations. He displays a knack for diffusing a mob in John 8:9 and comes up with creative ways out of accusations as in the taxes to Caesar incident in Matthew 22. And when he doesn't talk his way out of things, Jesus, like the 1930s radio character "The Shadow", seems to have the ability to "cloud men's minds" and just walk out of a crowd virtually unseen and untouched (see Luke 4:29–30). If worse came to worst, of course, he could blast a few fig trees and escape on foot over water, leaving all the sunglassed trackers and their sniffer dogs baying and howling, having lost the scent at the water's edge.

So how is it that the authorities trick him? How do his smooching betrayer and the temple guard manage to sneak up behind Jesus? Was it a momentary lapse in concentration? Did they lure him to their Jerusalem hideout with a kidnapped Mary Magdalene?

No. He does it all on purpose, with his eyes wide open. Jesus was clearer about this than anything else he talked about. The unfolding events are the result of a very deliberate decision on his part. Nor is there any sense of "Okay, I'm pretty much done now with the real work, the fireworks and healings and teaching. You basically got it; now it's time for me to mosey on down the line and make room for you, my brilliant students." Far from accepting his death now that his work is done, he regularly speaks as though the coming troubles are his real work, his central task.

When Jesus tells the boys that these things "must" happen, he doesn't mean it in a resigned Murphy's Law sort of way; the Greek construction is akin to the concepts of fate and destiny, but more personal. It has to be this way because it fits the will of the Creator. His response wouldn't have been, "Wouldn't you know it? Isn't that typical?"

I've made much in this book and in my previous one about how Jesus is always speaking in stories or in questions. When it comes to the very center of the gospel story, you and I would have him say, "Okay, you guys have been with me for a while. It's time I let you in on my secret identity: who I really am, what you're really dealing with." But the real Jesus asks (instead of tells), "Who do you say I am?"

But look at this: after Peter says, "You are the Christ", Jesus does not ask, "What do you think are the implications of that?" or "And what do you think the Christ's mission on earth is?" Instead, the gospels say, "He then began to teach them that the Son of Man must suffer many things and be rejected by the elders, the chief priests and the teachers of the law, and that he must be killed and after three days rise again." That's Mark 8:31. Lest there's any misunderstanding, Mark adds in the very next verse, "He spoke plainly about this." Matthew's gospel uses the word *explain*. Jesus explained this as he sometimes explained his parables. Here for a change is something he *tells* them rather than *asks* them. It's that important.

Of course, ironically, at the time, the disciples may not have realized that he was speaking plainly. They are used to him saying dramatic things that he doesn't mean literally: "From now on you will catch men instead of fish"; well, yes, figuratively speaking, but not literally with a bigger, stronger net. "I am the bread of life"; well, okay, metaphorically. So when he first told them that he would have to be put to death and would rise again, I'm sure they took this about the same way as when he told Nicodemus that he had to be born all over again.

Except for Peter, that is. Mark and Matthew both tell us that when he first heard about this, he not only took it literally but thought that Jesus was being unnecessarily pessimistic (see Matt. 16:22). "Ooh . . . negative energy, old pal. Buck up! You'll never amount to anything unless you learn to think positively. Repeat after me, Jesus: Just do it! I have the power! I'm worth it!"

Jesus sees any attempt at saving his life or circumventing his death not as an expression of faith and solidarity but as Satan's work. What a strong reaction—if this wasn't Jesus, you and I would read it and say, "Hey, there's no need to act like that!" Oh yes, there is. Jesus says he must suffer and die.

And it is after Peter's confession and this subsequent announcement that Jesus sets his face for this final fateful trip to Jerusalem. In John's gospel, the phrase that's emphasized in this whole business is "my hour". Jesus makes all kinds of statements about how his hour has not yet come and then, later, how his hour has come. The disciples, at that point, would have been clueless, probably assuming it to be the hour of his triumph as opposed to this traveling-around phase. With hindsight, however, we know that he means his impending death and resurrection. Jesus saw the center point of his life on earth, then, not as education, not as dialoguing and asking questions, not as healing, not as feeding crowds of people but as dying. Why? What possible use could he be to the sick and possessed and downhearted and oppressed if the Romans and Jerusalem officials are allowed to tack him up on their bulletin board, forcibly driving a wedge between his body and his spirit, ripping him in half for everyone to see? "Surely God won't let this happen to you!"

Suggestions for Further Thought

Have there ever been times in your life when well-meaning people tried to prevent you from doing something difficult that had to be done?

Reflect about how great God's love must be to have sent his Son here—knowing how it would have to turn out.

As a Ransom for Many

The Son of Man did not come to be served, but to serve, and to give his life as a ransom for many.

Mark 10:32-45

They were on their way up to Jerusalem, with Jesus leading the way, and the disciples were astonished, while those who followed were afraid. Again he took the Twelve aside and told them what was going to happen to him. "We are going up to Jerusalem," he said, "and the Son of Man will be delivered over to the chief priests and the teachers of the law. They will condemn him to death and will hand him over to the Gentiles, who will mock him and spit on him, flog him and kill him. Three days later he will rise."

Then James and John, the sons of Zebedee, came to him. "Teacher," they said, "we want you to do for us whatever we ask."

"What do you want me to do for you?" he asked.

They replied, "Let one of us sit at your right and the other at your left in your glory."

"You don't know what you are asking," Jesus said. "Can you drink the cup I drink or be baptized with the baptism I am baptized with?"

"We can," they answered.

Jesus said to them, "You will drink the cup I drink and be baptized with the baptism I am baptized with, but to sit at my right or left is not for me to grant. These places belong to those for whom they have been prepared."

When the ten heard about this, they became indignant with James and John. Jesus called them together and said, "You know that those who are regarded as rulers of the Gentiles lord it over them, and their high officials exercise authority over them. Not so with you. Instead, whoever wants to become great among you must be your servant, and whoever wants to be first must be slave of all. For even the Son of Man did not come to be served, but to serve, and to give his life as a ransom for many."

Suppose one of your friends told you that she "simply had to" run a marathon in a year's time. Okay, you might say, how can I help with the training or sponsorship or whatever? Well, she says, there's not much you can do. Then she tells you that the eighteenth mile is going to kill her. You gulp. But, she continues, she'll still get through it with a respectable time. Ah, you readjust your understanding of what your friend meant by "It's going to kill me." So what do you do next? Probably you either console your friend that the last nine miles won't be as hard as she expects, or you assure her that you'll be there on the finish line to celebrate with her.

That's the disciples. In the passage above, Jesus predicts his suffering and death. For all of us who know how the story is going to turn out, Jesus' words are perfectly plain. He's going to Jerusalem, he's going to suffer and die, he's going to rise from the dead. Where's the big mystery? Well, people don't just rise from the dead. As we saw last time, Jesus is always saying things with metaphors and images. I'm sure that when the disciples hear Jesus say he's going to suffer and die and rise again, some of them understand it along the lines of the marathon that will "kill" your friend. The gospels tell us that they discussed among themselves what he might have meant by the phrase "rising from the dead" (Mark 9:10). Some of them might have thought he was talking about something as serious as prison. Prisons were often underground, dark, cold places from which people tended not to emerge. Could Jesus have meant that he would be thrown into a prison "tomb", but the charges wouldn't stick? Or that there'd be a revolt and he'd be freed?

This is the third of the predictions in Mark. After every single one of them, the disciples react the wrong way. The first one is in Mark 8:31–33, where Peter objects to Jesus' prediction of suffering and is told, "Get behind me, Satan!" After the second prediction of suffering, death and resurrection in Mark 9:31, the following verses tell how the disciples were arguing among themselves about which of them would hold the highest rank in the New World Order they expect Jesus to bring about. Mark 10:32–45, the passage you've just read, follows directly from the third of Jesus' predictions in verses 33–34: "I'm going to Jerusalem to be condemned, flogged and killed. After three days I'll rise again." And then the Zebedee boys say, "Excellent. Can we have the top jobs?"

What is wrong with these guys? If you hear any sermons on these passages or read any books about them, the disciples are always given a really hard time for being so blind and stupid and self-centered.

Well, look again. They are being just like you and I would be. Think about it. They know that Jerusalem is going to be tough. But Jesus has told them that he will rise again (whatever he means by that), which means he'll be triumphant. Even their discussions about rank and what will happen afterward are based on their faith that Jesus is right—that he will be triumphant.

In other words, faced with a Jesus who says the race is going to kill him but he will get up and cross the finish line, the disciples do what anyone would do: try to assure him that the bad won't be that bad (Matt. 16:22) and then focus not on the difficult bit but on how great it will be to cross that finish line and celebrate.

For here is the very nub of the difference between the human perspective on the gospel story and the divine one. Left to our own devices, we see the suffering and cross as something that Jesus had to go through in order to get to the real event, the resurrection. Jesus triumphant, vindicated. It's only human to think his fate or destiny is to win and become king, no matter what adversities are thrown at him. Suffering and death (again, whatever he means by that) are hurdles or obstacles or distractions on the way to the finish line.

That's not the way Jesus sees it. And he has a heck of a time making it clear to his disciples that it is not about persevering through struggles to win at the end. He has come, not in order to rise, but in order to die. He is not running to come through with a respectable time; he is running in order to fall. Or rather the necessary centerpiece of the race he will run and complete is that falling (Heb. 12). To be sure, his death is not the end of the story, but it is the goal of the story, the whole point of the story. "The Son of Man did not come to be served, but to serve, and to give his life as a ransom for many" (Mark 10:45).

It is, of course, his suffering and death that he's referring to with the symbols of "his cup" and "his baptism" in Mark 10:38–40. The author does not use these symbols because they have by the time of writing become the church's sacraments. Rather, they become the sacraments for the same reason that they are apt symbols here: they are good Old Testament images of what God has in store for someone (Isa. 51:17; Ps. 23:5; 69:15). Suffering and death are what's in store for him (and for the Zebedee boys); Jesus' "hour" is not that bright Easter morning but the dark Friday evening.

When we start to think about what Jesus meant when he called his death a ransom, we're into pretty deep theological water. At this point we are little better off than the disciples. They too would have picked up the rich connections of ideas between Jesus' speech and the "servant song" of Isaiah 53—ideas including servanthood and ransom and the many. From the early days in their time with Jesus, the Galilean period, Jesus used Isaiah to describe his ministry according to Luke: "He has anointed me . . . to proclaim freedom for the prisoners . . . to release the oppressed" (Luke 4:18, Isa. 61:1–2). It seems that Jesus is now explaining how he will bring about that release. Contrary to first century expectations of the messiah, Jesus would not blast the Romans, but as in Isaiah 53, his own voluntary sufferings will do the business, the life of the servant will be a ransom.

Now a ransom is a payment made to secure the release of a captive or a slave. So far, so good. The traditional model forged by the church over the centuries is that Jesus' death is a once-and-for-all payment, which overcomes the effects of our sins and restores us into relationship with God. This model fits the New Testament evidence very well and is a fitting fulfilment of Old Testament images of sacrifices and atonement. But it is, of course, just a model: great for illustrating some facets of the real thing but possibly misleading about other facets. The divine reality of what Jesus accomplished is likely to be more vast than our abilities to describe it.

Pushing that imagery in unintended directions raises all sorts of difficulties. To whom would such a payment need to be made? Does it not imply that the recipient of the payment is otherwise unwilling to release the captive or slave? If so, then Satan is a candidate. But could God really be required to satisfy Satan before he is allowed to forgive and restore human beings? It might seem more likely that God is paying himself, punishing the innocent Son in place of guilty humanity so the accounts can be marked "paid". But then the whole drama seems to us unnecessarily and surreally complicated. "I love my humans. I want them back. But they've done wrong and deserve death. So I'll have to take the punishment and die in order to satisfy myself. But then I can raise myself from the dead and everyone will be happy again."

It is possible, of course, that our problems with it have more to do with our ability to comprehend than with this model. Some pretty clever and sensitive people throughout the centuries have imagined God having just such a conversation with himself and not thought it impossible. We live at a time and in a culture that has little notion of responsibility, much less sin; a culture whose notions of justice are derived not from what is right but from individuals' rights and economic expediency. In such a culture, it is understandable that some today find the implications of this model unhelpful, distasteful and difficult to communicate. It may be that evangelism can no longer focus exclusively on a cross that culture has rendered unintelligible (though that didn't stop Paul in similar conditions in Corinth).

The gospel is bigger than any of our attempts to explain it. But I'll tell you what: the bits of the gospel we most need to hear and contemplate are not likely to be the ones that dovetail neatly with what our non-Christian culture teaches us. We should expect a message from above not only to confirm the good things in our background but also to cut across and contradict our agreed common sense. Those are the hardest truths to learn—like meeting the rightful King and learning that he has not come to claim his throne. At least not in the usual way.

Suggestions for Further Thought

Some people find it helpful to think about the cross in this way: Jesus became a model of submissive obedience—a refusal to give into the sin of answering human violence with violence. Recognizing that no model is complete, how would this one help us to share the truth of Jesus with people today?

Just as some non-Christians think the Trinity means that Christians believe in three gods, some people find the cross difficult, thinking it implies two gods—good cop, bad cop—an angry Judge-God looking for someone to punish and an innocent Jesus-God defusing that angry God on our behalf. How can we be careful to avoid this kind of miscommunication?

The Last Supper

This is my blood of the covenant, which is poured out for many for the forgiveness of sins.

Matthew 26:17–30

On the first day of the Festival of Unleavened Bread, the disciples came to Jesus and asked, "Where do you want us to make preparations for you to eat the Passover?"

He replied, "Go into the city to a certain man and tell him, 'The Teacher says: My appointed time is near. I am going to celebrate the Passover with my disciples at your house.'" So the disciples did as Jesus had directed them and prepared the Passover.

When evening came, Jesus was reclining at the table with the Twelve. And while they were eating, he said, "Truly I tell you, one of you will betray me."

They were very sad and began to say to him one after the other, "Surely not I, Lord?"

Jesus replied, "The one who has dipped his hand into the bowl with me will betray me. The Son of Man will go just as it is written about him. But woe to that man who betrays the Son of Man! It would be better for him if he had not been born."

Then Judas, the one who would betray him, said, "Surely not I, Rabbi?"

Jesus answered, "You have said so."

While they were eating, Jesus took bread, and when he had given thanks, he broke it and gave it to his disciples, saying, "Take and eat; this is my body."

Then he took the cup, and when he had given thanks, he gave it to them, saying, "Drink from it, all of you. This is my blood of the covenant, which is poured out for many for the forgiveness of sins. I tell you, I will not drink of this fruit of the vine from now on until that day when I drink it new with you in my Father's kingdom."

When they had sung a hymn, they went out to the Mount of Olives.

Then Jesus told them, "This very night you will all fall away on account of me, for it is written:

" 'I will strike the shepherd,
and the sheep of the flock will be scattered.' "

The disciples have a secret agent thing going in Mark's version of the story (14:12–16). Look for a guy doing women's work, carrying a water jug, follow him and give him the secret password: "The Teacher asks, 'Where is my guest room?'" Maybe this is meant as a supernatural voice of command event—"These are not the droids we're looking for." More likely it indicates some advance planning and a network of Jesus' supporters in the city.

In any case, a room has been prepared. Two details make it clear we're talking about the actual Passover meal. Normally, the final meal of the day would be in the afternoon. Normally, Jesus and his gang would have left the city to spend the evening in Bethany, outside Jerusalem. (You may remember the fig tree cursing incident, which happened on the commute.) Today we're told that they're all staying in town and eating in the evening (Matt. 26:20) and that this is a special celebration: Passover.

You don't have to be Jewish to know about Passover, but it helps. Even Gentiles know it's an annual festival meal, full of reminders of the captivity in Egypt and God liberating his people in the exodus. So you've got bitter herbs, which speak of slavery, and unleavened bread, because the departure from Egypt was in such haste, and so on.

But for religious Jews it goes beyond symbolism and a time to be with family and friends. It is, in some ways, an actual participation in the mysteries of God's acting and delivering, and an expression of solidarity with our ancestors through the ages. Remembering the bitter years of slavery and making bricks without straw under Pharaoh, we don't say "when our forefathers were in Egypt", we say "when we were in Egypt".

Arguably, Passover is the most important Jewish holiday just as the exodus is the most important event in Jewish history. How much chutzpah, how much nerve would it take to hijack this holiday? "Never mind Moses and the exodus and the whole basis of our faith, I've got something important to tell you about."

Well guess what? Jesus has a lot of nerve. He and the gang go into that upstairs room for a Passover meal, and what do his followers remember best and think most important? A new set of imagery for the meal's most ordinary elements: the bread and the wine.

And not only has he changed the meal to commemorate an event other than the exodus, namely his death, but this first "remembrance" meal happens before the event it commemorates. It shares this property with the first Passover meal. That meal was instituted and the sacrificed lamb's blood sprinkled on the doorposts to ward away the plague of death. How laden the Lord's Supper is with exodus harmonies and overtones. Or is it the other way around?

Actually, though, there is some controversy surrounding the identification of the Last Supper with the Passover meal or at least with Passover evening proper. Although the gospels make it quite plain Jesus and the disciples prepared a Passover supper for the upper room, John's gospel makes it sound as though Jesus was being crucified just when the Passover lambs were being slaughtered for Passover celebrations. In that case the Last Supper must have taken place the night before. So was it a proper Passover or not?

Although this is sometimes made out to be a "gospel contradiction" and trotted out as an argument against trusting the Bible, there are many possible explanations for the two different perspectives—too many to be positive about which one is correct.

My colleague Steve Motyer, in his little book *Remember Jesus*, comes up with a most interesting suggestion. John's timing is correct, Steve argues, but Jesus, knowing what would happen, decided to celebrate the Passover with his disciples a night early.

Now here's where the plot thickens: celebrating a night early means having the meal the night before the lambs were slaughtered. In other words, they're eating supper, but the main course isn't there on the platter, steaming, but out on the grass, bleating. Remember, this is no ordinary main course, but the one where you ate the meat and sprinkled the blood to protect the family from death. No protecting blood, no sacrificed flesh at this "day before" sitting of the meal, then, right?

Wrong. Jesus picks up the bread and says it is flesh, picks up the wine and says it is blood. There's no unblemished lamb for Christ's followers except Jesus himself. What was it John the Baptist said so early in the going? "Look, the Lamb of God, who takes away the sin of the world!" (John 1:29).

Whether the meal happened with or without lamb on the table, for the first believers the central feast of Judaism morphed into the central rite of Christianity. Did Jesus mean for Passover celebrations to cease? Did he mean to replace that with this? Rather than the foundational deliverance from the slavery in Egypt, we celebrate the timeless deliverance from something similar but bigger. And rather than an animal's blood that saves us, it is Jesus' blood.

And his blood is all tied up with his willing acceptance of the incarnation—God become flesh. According to John 6:35–58, Jesus talked about this long before, and in terms that must have shocked his hearers. "Very truly I tell you, unless you eat the flesh of the Son of Man and drink his blood, you have no life in you" (v. 53). No cultural sensitivity here! In the Last Supper, Jesus at last shows his disciples how to understand and practice what sounds an absurd and gruesome business.

The gospel writers love to stack the four verbs here. The words were for them and as they are for us—at every communion service, the perfect encapsulation of the incarnation. He took up human flesh, thereby blessing it anew, and allowed it to be broken so it could be given to everyone. Those four verbs—take, bless, break and give—are also used to describe the miraculous feeding of the 5,000 and again, significantly, after the resurrection, when the two disciples recognize him after meeting him on the road to Emmaus in Luke 24.

Okay, I admit it: molding this book around meals and eating is schmaltzy. But it's not without precedent. The church has always related to Jesus this way. You see it as early as the epistles. Neither Paul nor the other letter writers tell long stories about what Jesus said or what Jesus did. No long parables, no extended quotations from the Sermon on the Mount, no retellings of any miracles or anything like that. There is only one longish passage in the epistles, 1 Corinthians 11, which comes from the gospel material. In it Paul recommends that since the Corinthians' current worship services are doing "more harm than good" (11:17), they need to cut back on all their current focus on self-expression and concentrate on the Lord's Supper. They are not to regard it as an ordinary meal of ordinary food (11:20–22). Instead, years before our gospels were written, Paul recites for them again the tradition he received and passed on to them before, the words both he and his churches probably recited in the church's weekly liturgy:

> For I received from the Lord what I also passed on to you: The Lord Jesus, on the night he was betrayed, took bread, and when he had given thanks, he broke it and said, "This is my body, which is for you; do this in remembrance of me." In the same way, after supper he took the cup, saying, "This cup is the new covenant in my blood; do this, whenever you drink it, in remembrance of me. " For whenever you eat this bread and drink this cup, you proclaim the Lord's death until he comes.
>
> 1 Corinthians 11:23—26

In the account in John 13, before the meal, Jesus washed the disciples' feet. He told them earlier he had not come to be served but to serve (Mark 10:45). He had come not to be sacrificed for, but to be a sacrifice. Not only to provide food but to become our food. His purpose was not merely to announce or provide deliverance and salvation but to become deliverance and salvation for us.

Look! The Lamb of God!

Suggestions for Further Thought

How frequently does your church or fellowship celebrate the Lord's Supper? When you do, is it the center of worship or an afterthought? How can you make it more central?

Imagine yourself at that hut in Emmaus when the "stranger" becomes the host. Try writing a few paragraphs about how you recognize Jesus when he takes, blesses, breaks and gives—why those actions?

The Garden at the Center of Time

"*Abba*, Father," he said, "everything is possible for you. Take this cup from me. Yet not what I will, but what you will."

Mark 14:32–42

They went to a place called Gethsemane, and Jesus said to his disciples, "Sit here while I pray." He took Peter, James and John along with him, and he began to be deeply distressed and troubled. "My soul is overwhelmed with sorrow to the point of death," he said to them. "Stay here and keep watch."

Going a little farther, he fell to the ground and prayed that if possible the hour might pass from him. "*Abba*, Father," he said, "everything is possible for you. Take this cup from me. Yet not what I will, but what you will."

Then he returned to his disciples and found them sleeping. "Simon," he said to Peter, "are you asleep? Could you not keep watch for one hour? Watch and pray so that you will not fall into temptation. The spirit is willing, but the flesh is weak."

Once more he went away and prayed the same thing. When he came back, he again found them sleeping, because their eyes were heavy. They did not know what to say to him.

Returning the third time, he said to them, "Are you still sleeping and resting? Enough! The hour has come. Look, the Son of Man is delivered into the hands of sinners. Rise! Let us go! Here comes my betrayer!"

his is no prayer meeting. It's more like the deployment of troops. After supper, the disciples are brought to Gethsemane and told, "Sit here." Then Jesus' favorites—Peter, James and John—are brought farther in. Only to these three, Jesus opens his heart: he's in anguish. Even so, they don't get to pray with him. They're told to stay and keep watch. Jesus goes on a little farther to pray by himself. As we've seen earlier, it's not unusual for him to pray alone; what's unusual is for him to want company and arrange to have it close at hand. Later, Jesus chastises the three for snoozing on the job.

The passage reminds me of two others. One is the transfiguration, especially in Luke. Both events center around supernatural conversations and focus on Jesus' death (Luke 9:30–31). There too Jesus left the Twelve behind except for the same three favorites to witness him praying (Luke 9:28) and they became drowsy (v. 32). Then as now, the disciples didn't quite know what to say (v. 33).

That's straightforward. The other parallel troubles me more. Back in Mark 4:37–41 the disciples faced what they regarded as their hour of need, a terrible squall on the lake. They turned to Jesus for help but found him asleep. Exasperated, they demanded, "Don't you care if we drown?"

This is why it troubles me. In the garden, how does Jesus have the nerve to browbeat his disciples, sleeping in a quiet garden in the night, when he himself slept through a storm at sea in a small boat?

And here's another thing: he exhorts the sleepyheads to watch and pray to avoid falling into temptation. What temptation? Merely the temptation to sleep?

Before trying to answer these things, we should consider the passage's center: Jesus at prayer.

We have the content of Jesus' prayer in the garden. Or at least we have a summary. The two or three sentences the gospels give us take only a few seconds to say, barely time for dozy disciples to fluff up the pillows, much less fall asleep.

It's unlikely he spent the time repeating these few sentences over and over like some late-twentieth century gospel chorus. So what can we tell about what he did pray from this summary?

Mark's version is the oldest and fullest. From it we can guess at the way Jesus' conversation with his Father may have gone. After our earlier discussion about Jesus' prayers, the pattern will sound familiar.

The prayer begins with "*Abba*, Father" (Mark 14:36; "My Father" in Matthew's version, 26:39), a phrase that, as we've seen, speaks volumes about the special relationship. It begins the whole interaction by affirming Jesus' love and devotion. It's tempting to think this section would have been expanded in the unrecorded whole prayer, but perhaps not realistic to expect too much; Jesus has spoken to the three about his distress, it's not unlikely his prayer moved quickly to that.

Mark's version reveals a struggle in prayer, almost an argument. "Father, everything is possible for you. Take this cup from me" (Mark 14:36). How very like some contemporary discussions of Jesus' atonement this seems! God can do anything; how can he be unable to provide a blood-free forgiveness—one, in the words of the late Douglas Adams, in which "no one would have to get nailed to anything"? This is no new question: people have been wrestling with the offensive nature of the cross since at least the night before it happened! Jesus and the biblical writers faced it head on, argued it out not only with each other but with God.

I wouldn't be surprised if this section is the most condensed in the gospels' summary of this realistic and human prayer: Here's what I want, God, here's why it's not a crazy thing to ask for. You can do anything you want, so please spare me from this!

But there's one more sentence in the summary, a sentence that changes everything. It's reported almost identically by the gospel writers: "Yet not what I will, but what you will" (Mark 14:36; cf. Matt. 26:39; Luke 22:42). This should bring to mind the Lord's Prayer, which Jesus gave the disciples as a model, and may be standing in for a longer time at prayer, which included much of the Lord's Prayer. The garden prayer session as a whole echoes the pattern set up by the Lord's Prayer.

What is intensified and sharpened here, though, is something left unspecified in the Lord's Prayer: what do we do when it is not God's will to "deliver us from evil" or "give us this day our daily bread" in the way we wish it?

Here is the attitude God wants from us all. In this world, I don't think he wants followers who go along with every circumstance without question. It is not wrong for Jesus (and for us) to push back at him: you can do anything; why not do this? Not that he wants people whose main attitude is pushing back, but who combine the questioning with a willingness to back off and trust him to do what's best. Secular thinkers often flatter themselves unjustly: the difference between faith and doubt is not in the quality or even the frequency of the questions. The difference is whether, when the crunch comes, one trusts in oneself and one's own questions or the other and his trustworthiness. Self or other? It's that simple. If I don't understand it—can't see it—must it then be wrong?

Wouldn't you have thought a religiously together person would avoid praying for something he knew God didn't want? Wouldn't you say once God said no, the good little Christian should say, "Okay, Lord. Sorry I asked"? Think again. This isn't how the exemplary religious person, Jesus, acts. Having gone through these three stages—(1) affirming the relationship, (2) questioning and pushing back on the specifics, (3) acknowledging God's will over his own— he did not get off his knees and get on with life cheerfully, everything hunky-dory. Look at Mark 14:39: "Once more he went away and prayed the same thing." Once more, and from the top! Jesus prays for it not once, not twice, but three times. And he prays for it, apparently, already having some sense it is not going to happen.

It's unlikely the prayers are word-for-word the same, mind you. Matthew 26:39 and 42 may indicate a progression. The first time, Jesus' prayer goes like this: "All things are possible. Take it away. Nevertheless, your will, not mine." The second time, there's a subtle difference; it's more concessive: "If it's not possible to take it away, may your will be done."

Don't make too much of this difference. Despite it, the gospel writers are willing to say Jesus prayed the same thing. The questioning and request phase is not gone—Jesus doesn't switch to a psalm praising God whose inscrutable purposes are greater than anyone can imagine. Yet the early disjunction between the request section and the submission section is softening and the distinct phases have become connected: not "It's possible. Take it away. Nevertheless, your will be done" but "If it's not possible to take it away, then your will be done."

It's not only Jesus who displays this pattern either. Remember Paul's thorn in the flesh? He says, "Three times I pleaded with the Lord to take it away from me. But he said to me, 'My grace is sufficient for you, for my power is made perfect in weakness'" (2 Cor. 12:8–9). Three times, again! New Testament prayer is not about "wish fulfilment" but about seeking harmony between two wills and the sometimes hard-won acceptance and trust of the one will over the other.

I have called Gethsemane the garden at the center of time because the crisis of the cross is the center of God's interaction with us human beings. The central matter of the cross is not merely in the dying, nor even in dying and rising, but in submission, dying and rising. In the garden we see the climax and conclusion of the first movement of the symphony.

Since the first snack break in Eden, there has been no more important chain of events in human history. Yet the three hand-picked witnesses—Peter, James and John—are nodding off rather than watching as they were told.

"Watch and pray so that you will not fall into temptation. The spirit is willing, but the flesh is weak" (Mark 14:38). So was this the temptation: zonking out rather than keeping alert? Hmmm . . . that would mean Jesus was saying, "Watch and pray so you will watch and not sleep", or "Watch so you're not tempted to stop watching." That doesn't seem quite right. I think there's another temptation here. Luke tells us the three were not just tired from a long day and a late supper. He says they were "exhausted from sorrow" (Luke 22:45).

Jesus' response to this exhaustion in Luke is, "Get up and pray so that you will not fall into temptation" (22:46). Perhaps the victory they are to win through prayer is the same as his. He too came to prayer "overwhelmed with sorrow" (Mark 14:34). Through prayer, he ensured his will became conformed to his Father's. As we've seen, throughout the gospels the disciples balked at Jesus' coming death. At that parallel passage, the transfiguration, they seem to want to erect some structures rather than move on to the danger he predicted in Jerusalem. We all know how they fled and hid after his arrest. Is the temptation they're to avoid this unworked-through sorrow, the temptation to stay in despair? Watch and pray so you don't fall into despair—pray to bring your wills into line. Is this what's going on?

If so, it helps me with my troubles about the sleeping through the storm story I mentioned at the start. In fact, it helps me understand both passages better. In the earlier story, even though it was the disciples who were awake and it was Jesus who slept, they displayed this same temptation to despair: "Don't you care if we drown!" In return, Jesus asks them, "Do you still have no faith?"

(Mark 4:38–40) Then and now in the garden, they need to learn to pray as Jesus did. It's not a calm, confident prayer, but neither does it stop at despair— "We'll all be killed!"

Faith does not shelve the questions, or hide objections to the way things are. Faith is about wrestling with those questions and objections. Faith is not stopping short of the questions and the despair; faith is about moving past them as Jesus did in his prayer in the garden at the center of time. Everything turns upon this attitude of Jesus in Gethsemane, and the way he acts on it (through the trial and crucifixion) and the way his Father acts on it (on Easter morning).

Suggestions for Further Thought

How could the second person of the Trinity even think about questioning the cross and going against the will of God?

Think of some child you know, offspring or cousin or niece/nephew, and some concern or desire that they might approach you with. How would they display to you the different attitudes of (1) robotic submission, (2) arrogant insistence and (3) the pushing-back but submissive attitude of Jesus? Now, which attitude is most like the way you act with authorities and with God?

A Tale of Two Wash Basins

"Where do you come from?" he asked Jesus, but Jesus gave him no answer. "Do you refuse to speak to me?" Pilate said. "Don't you realize I have power either to free you or to crucify you?"

John 18:29–19:16

So Pilate came out to them and asked, "What charges are you bringing against this man?"

"If he were not a criminal," they replied, "we would not have handed him over to you."

Pilate said, "Take him yourselves and judge him by your own law."

"But we have no right to execute anyone," they objected. This took place to fulfill what Jesus had said about the kind of death he was going to die.

Pilate then went back inside the palace, summoned Jesus and asked him, "Are you the king of the Jews?"

"Is that your own idea," Jesus asked, "or did others talk to you about me?"

"Am I a Jew?" Pilate replied. "Your own people and chief priests handed you over to me. What is it you have done?"

Jesus said, "My kingdom is not of this world. If it were, my servants would fight to prevent my arrest by the Jewish leaders. But now my kingdom is from another place."

"You are a king, then!" said Pilate.

Jesus answered, "You say that I am a king. In fact, the reason I was born and came into the world is to testify to the truth. Everyone on the side of truth listens to me."

"What is truth?" retorted Pilate. With this he went out again to the Jews gathered there and said, "I find no basis for a charge against him. But it is your custom for me to release to you one prisoner at the time of the Passover. Do you want me to release 'the king of the Jews'?"

They shouted back, "No, not him! Give us Barabbas!" Now Barabbas had taken part in an uprising.

Then Pilate took Jesus and had him flogged. The soldiers twisted together a crown of thorns and put it on his head. They clothed him in a purple robe and went up to him again and again, saying, "Hail, king of the Jews!" And they slapped him in the face.

Once more Pilate came out and said to the Jews, "Look, I am bringing him out to you to let you know that I find no basis for a charge against him." When Jesus came out wearing the crown of thorns and the purple robe, Pilate said to them, "Here is the man!"

As soon as the chief priests and their officials saw him, they shouted, "Crucify! Crucify!"

But Pilate answered, "You take him and crucify him. As for me, I find no basis for a charge against him."

The Jews insisted, "We have a law, and according to that law he must die, because he claimed to be the Son of God."

When Pilate heard this, he was even more afraid, and he went back inside the palace. "Where do you come from?" he asked Jesus, but Jesus gave him no answer. "Do you refuse to speak to me?" Pilate said. "Don't you realize I have power either to free you or to crucify you?"

Jesus answered, "You would have no power over me if it were not given to you from above. Therefore the one who handed me over to you is guilty of a greater sin."

From then on, Pilate tried to set Jesus free, but the Jews kept shouting, "If you let this man go, you are no friend of Caesar. Anyone who claims to be a king opposes Caesar."

When Pilate heard this, he brought Jesus out and sat down on the judge's seat at a place known as the Stone Pavement (which in Aramaic is Gabbatha). It was the day of Preparation of the Passover; it was about noon.

"Here is your king," Pilate said to the Jews.

But they shouted, "Take him away! Take him away! Crucify him!"

"Shall I crucify your king?" Pilate asked.

"We have no king but Caesar," the chief priests answered.

Finally Pilate handed him over to them to be crucified.

So the soldiers took charge of Jesus.

The trial and incarceration of Jesus of Nazareth was a horrible business: Jewish false witnesses, twisting Jesus' words and swearing blind that Jesus was plotting against the temple; the Roman soldiers, crowning him with thorns, blindfolding him and telling him to use his supernatural insight to tell them who slugged him. It doesn't help much that many of the key players were only doing what they saw as their duty.

For the Jewish political leadership, it was a bit of self-regulation. They hoped to keep their country safe from Roman force by showing they didn't support uprisings and popular anti-heroes. If the guy was not going to succeed against the Romans, the Jews themselves would be better off to cut him down than allow the Romans an excuse to fully mobilize.

As far as the religious element goes, Christians often seem unable to realize Jesus did make blasphemous claims. If anyone but God incarnate had said and done the things this man said and did, any Jewish religious leader who did not denounce him and try to stop him would be neglecting his duty.

They tried hard to nail him on charges connected to the temple. This is a bit like putting the gangster Al Capone away for "income tax evasion". Because the Romans had to give their okay to any proposed death penalty, it was wisest to convict criminals, whatever their true offences, on a crime the Romans understood. They understood temples and temple violation. That's why the false witnesses were told to testify concerning Jesus' remarks about the temple — it would have made for an easy conviction. Later in the New Testament, the temple features prominently in the accusations against the martyr Stephen and the apostle Paul. It was a good PR move as well; it was easier to get the crowds riled up against Jesus by saying he insulted the temple than by saying he insulted some Pharisees and Sadducees! The failure to maintain this charge meant they'd go to Pilate with Jesus' implicit claims to kingship and loyalty instead.

It's hard to blame even the guards for their cruelty. It was not their job to second-guess the law courts regarding guilt or innocence. It was their job to make troublemakers into an object lesson, to deter others from becoming troublemakers. For the guards to treat him politely would have been counterproductive from their point of view. Everyone was doing their duty.

At this point it's traditional for the author (that's me) to have a go at the "fickle" crowds, who are all "Hosanna!" one minute and "Crucify!" the next.

But even if they are the same people, they've seen and heard quite a bit in between those two occasions and they don't know all we know. What they've seen is a gang who marched into the city, accepted their praises, their leader a man who fearlessly swept the commercial elements out of the temple. But as the days went by, they began to see this leader as a flash in the pan. He not only has been rejected by the leadership and lost to the Romans, but has allowed himself to be totally humiliated. The crowds, understandably, wanted someone to defy the authorities, both Jewish and Roman. But at this stage of his life, Jesus before his opponents turned silent as a sheep before its shearers. Should the crowds, who have barely met him, remain loyal when even his close followers have deserted their leader and gone into hiding? They'd hoped for a lion, not one who like a lamb would allow himself to be led to slaughter. I wouldn't call that fickle; they probably called it "being willing to admit they'd been wrong about this so-called Deliverer from Nazareth". They had seen it all before. In fact, some previous Galilean rebels were more spectacular. At first glance, precious little would have made Jesus different; precious little that couldn't be explained as something spiritual you thought you perceived. If what you wanted in a messiah were "relevance" and "something that makes a difference in the real world", wouldn't you have turned against him at this point?

As for Pilate, he hoped to show himself a governor who kept the peace in a difficult land and guarded his emperor's prerogatives. His job was full of compromises. Think about it from his perspective: he saw nothing wrong with the common people worshiping the emperor. They did. He tried explaining it. They were still against it. Fine, they were excused from worshiping the emperor. Case closed; what's next? They thought this man worthy of death. Pilate didn't. He tried some alternatives. They didn't go for them. Fine, have him put to death! Next case.

Except he somehow knew Jesus didn't deserve death. Was there something about Jesus that tipped it off to Pilate? John's gospel tells us more about their conversations together than the other gospels. Jesus tells Pilate his kingdom is not of this world, and Pilate quips, "What is truth?" Did Jesus' words get to him? Or is it the dignity he finds in Jesus' composure and silence? Does Pilate intuitively understand Jesus' depths and find him innocent with a capital *I*? I find it even more tempting, though, to think Pilate misreads Jesus completely and finds him harmless with a lowercase *h*. Pilate would have found it easier to read Jesus' accusers (with whom he would have had prior dealings). Why are the Sanhedrin so anxious—too anxious—to ensure a Roman end for one of their own people—complete with trumped-up charges about Jesus' claims to royalty and opposition to taxes?

Nevertheless, there is a kinship between the two; both are leaders, both have come to Israel for a time from somewhere else, on loan by an emperor for specific tasks. But their leadership styles could hardly have been more different. Jesus once attempted to acquit someone from judgement—a woman caught in adultery. Having made up his mind, he took his time, then stood his ground. He confronted the mob, defusing it by decisively demanding they consider their own sinlessness before casting the first stone (John 8:7).

By comparison, Pilate's attempts on Jesus' behalf were the pathetic, half-hearted efforts of a coward—sneaking him in to be released at the Feast, shunting him off to Herod. "You don't really want to kill him, do you? You do? Oh, well, have him then." Pilate always looks to stand above it all, whereas Jesus would jump into the thick of it. Pilate was, after all, a politician. As such, he would have had one eye to an imaginary mirror: How will this look? How will it play to the real audience back home? What are the implications for career advancement?

This was Jesus' hour; this was the reason he came. He did not, it has to be said, give his judges much grounds on which to release him. He does not try to get free, does not reply to charges with airtight defenses. No turning-the-tables parables, no crushingly clever rejoinders, he's like a different guy now. Instead, he seems to mutter oblique assents that boil down to "If you say so". His hour has come, and he neither hastens it nor makes any further attempt to ward it off. Why quibble about it with the likes of the Jewish Supreme Court or the Roman governor when he has argued it all through the night before in the garden with the only authority who matters?

Remember Obi-Wan Kenobi in the first Star Wars film? At one point in the big duel, he unlights his light sabre and stands defenseless but confident before Darth Vader, saying sonorously, "If you strike me down, I shall become more powerful than you can possibly imagine." Jesus stands still a lot longer than that, and he is in for much more complete punishment and humiliation than a quick flick of an energy beam. But he's also not doing it in order to become more powerful. Tolkien understood the concept better. When Gandalf sacrificed himself, coming back in a bright new suit was the furthest thing from his mind. He was thinking about the people he was saving and what he was saving them from.

Earth said no to Jesus. Both Pilate and Jesus faced up to that rejection over their wash basins. Pilate washed his hands; Jesus washed his disciples' feet. Therein lies all the difference between human ideas of government and God's.

So they took Jesus away. And he let them.

Suggestions for Further Thought

Imagine yourself at the back of the crowd. This Jesus, who had won you over initially into believing that he would champion your cause against the fascist, dictatorial empire, was now a submissive docile prisoner—making no defiant last stand from the platform. Even his closest followers were nowhere to be found. What would it take to make you stick by Jesus, contrary to the crowd and to the evidence?

In *The Lion, the Witch and the Wardrobe*, on the eve of Aslan's death, he and Peter plot out the battle with the Witch after his sacrifice to pay for Edmund's betrayal. Aslan tells Peter he cannot guarantee he will be part of that battle, as if he's not sure about his own resurrection. Has C. S. Lewis gone too far in emphasizing the death over the resurrection—should Aslan say, in Arnie's voice, "I'll be back"?

The Cross

Darkness came over the whole land . . . [and] Jesus cried out in a loud voice, . . . "My God, my God, why have you forsaken me?"

Mark 15:25–41

It was nine in the morning when they crucified him. The written notice of the charge against him read: THE KING OF THE JEWS. They crucified two rebels with him, one on his right and one on his left. Those who passed by hurled insults at him, shaking their heads and saying, "So! You who are going to destroy the temple and build it in three days, come down from the cross and save yourself!"

In the same way the chief priests and the teachers of the law mocked him among themselves. "He saved others," they said, "but he can't save himself! Let this Messiah, this king of Israel, come down now from the cross, that we may see and believe." Those crucified with him also heaped insults on him.

At noon, darkness came over the whole land until three in the afternoon. And at three in the afternoon Jesus cried out in a loud voice, "*Eloi, Eloi, lema sabachthani?*" (which means "My God, my God, why have you forsaken me?"). When some of those standing near heard this, they said, "Listen, he's calling Elijah."

Someone ran, filled a sponge with wine vinegar, put it on a staff, and offered it to Jesus to drink. "Now leave him alone. Let's see if Elijah comes to take him down," he said.

With a loud cry, Jesus breathed his last.

The curtain of the temple was torn in two from top to bottom. And when the centurion, who stood there in front of Jesus, saw how he died, he said, "Surely this man was the Son of God!"

Some women were watching from a distance. Among them were Mary Magdalene, Mary the mother of James the younger and of Joseph, and Salome.

In Galilee these women had followed him and cared for his needs. Many other women who had come up with him to Jerusalem were also there.

esus' experience on the cross must have been horrific. I'd guess most of you reading this have heard the sermons about crucifixion, maybe even seen the standard Roman nails and been forced to imagine those nine-inch spikes going through a wrist. You may have seen Mel Gibson's film of the passion. But it wasn't only physical torture Jesus experienced.

To be despised by the Romans was expected. To be rejected by his own nation was tragic. To be betrayed, denied and abandoned by his best friends must have hurt as much as the flogging. But Jesus was not a man who would confuse how things were going with how God was feeling about him. He's the guy who said, "Blessed are you when people insult you, persecute you and falsely say all kinds of evil against you . . . Rejoice and be glad, because great is your reward in heaven, for in the same way they persecuted the prophets who were before you" (Matt. 5:10–12). Going by this, if it were just the Romans, Jews and disciples rejecting him, Jesus should have died a painful but confident death, sure of his reward in heaven and the Father's praise.

So when, instead, Jesus cries out, "My God, why have you forsaken me?" it is likely he's doing more than looking at his situation and concluding God's rejection from that. There must have been a real, not just implied, rending of the relationship at that point. He, who did not deserve it, drank the cup he wished would pass away—the cup of the wrath and displeasure of God. That would have cut more keenly and deeply than all the other rejections combined.

This was the cup he'd wrestled with accepting in the garden, the culmination of his mission on earth. Everything he'd done and said was predicated on or aimed at this. And, Christians believe, not only his life, but all human history, especially the history of our relationship with God, aims at the cross and God's sacrifice of his own. Strike this chord and the whole Bible resonates with it. Passages bounce up and down clamoring for attention, from the pages of Genesis where, for instance, the snake is told he will strike the heel of the woman's offspring but that heel will crush the snake's head, or where God provides Abraham on the mountaintop with a sacrifice that will serve instead of the blood of Abraham's own son. Isaiah, thinking of his people's lowest ebb, also contemplates God's irony in chapter 53, writing centuries before Jesus' cross was slid into its upright position on the Hill of Skulls:

> "He was despised and rejected by men,
> a man of sorrows, and familiar with suffering.
> Like one from whom men hide their faces
> he was despised, and we esteemed him not.
> Surely he took up our infirmities
> and carried our sorrows,
> yet we considered him stricken by God,
> smitten by him, and afflicted.
> But he was pierced for our transgressions,
> he was crushed for our iniquities;
> The punishment that brought us peace was upon him,
> and by his wounds we are healed.
> We all, like sheep, have gone astray,
> each of us has turned to his own way;
> and the LORD has laid on him
> the iniquity of us all."
>
> Isaiah 53:3–6

It reaches from the beginning of the Bible all the way to the end in the book of Revelation. Surprisingly, it isn't "Worthy is the Lamb who lived a sinless life" or "Worthy is the Lamb who told spiritually enlightening stories." Instead it is, "Worthy is the Lamb who was slain!"

Looking back over the whole of this book, we've seen various facets of Jesus' life and ministry, beginning with his role as a teacher. It is in the light of the cross (or should that be in the darkness of the cross?) that we understand where all his teaching was headed. I'm not just thinking about his explicit sayings about how it was necessary for Messiah to go to Jerusalem in order to suffer and die, although that was an important strand in his teaching. I'm also thinking about themes such as not resisting evil and turning the other cheek; the way one has to trust that the Father is watching and will take care to do what is best. How chilling at this stage to contemplate the once comforting passages. Not even a sparrow falls from the sky without God taking notice. But sparrows do fall from the sky.

He also taught about not coming to be served but to serve; he is the servant of all. His teaching on humility and self-sacrifice blends into another facet we've focused on in the book: those aspects of his life that we might group together under the heading Spirituality. As ever in this realm, Jesus' self-sacrifice is at once a fierce adherence to scriptural Jewish spirituality and a radical protest against it demonstrating the bankruptcy of the current state of Jewish religious practice. He gives himself up. But his lifelong practice of living toward God is most visible here on the cross. He prays some bitter prayers, but even when feeling abandoned by God, he expresses that *to God* in words that come from the Scriptures (Ps. 22:1).

But what about the important strand of his miracles and healings? Those mighty powers seem to have deserted him on the cross as well. Has God withdrawn the power that seemed to flow through Jesus so readily, almost unconsciously, during his travels in Galilee?

There are two answers. The first comes in the sayings of the bystanders whom we find in Mark 15:31, making sarcastic cracks like, "Oh, right, he can save everyone else, but he cannot save himself." They spoke more truly than they knew, for that was the exact point Jesus was trying to get across to the disciples all along. He had to go to Jerusalem and die not because he hadn't the power to walk through the midst of his accusers unseen, not because he hadn't the power to heal his flogged back, not because he isn't stronger than death, but because dying was his mission. To save others precisely by not saving himself. Not to save himself, though he could, but to save others, which was much, much harder.

We find this same principle in one of Jesus' first acts: withstanding Satan's temptations. One of those temptations was miraculous feeding. "Make bread for yourself! It cannot be wrong to eat when you're so hungry." And Jesus would not. Later, he goes in for supernatural feedings in a big way, miraculously supplying bread like crazy. What changed? Others he could feed; himself he would not feed. He came not to be served, not even by himself, but to serve.

That's answer number one. What's answer number two? Wait three days.

Suggestions for Further Thought

If Disney had gotten hold of the story, we would have sparkly special effects envelop Jesus on the cross. Behind him the cross would shatter into a zillion slow-motion pieces as Jesus lands on the ground in a three-point crouch, then straightens up to a swell of triumphant John Williams-esque music. Cut to fleeing centurions. Now *there's* a Christ we could sell to people today! How do you reconcile the tension between Christ the Victor and Christ the Victim in the biblical version?

Should we call it Good Friday or Bad Friday?

Missing? The Women at the Tomb

He is not here.

Luke 24:1–12

On the first day of the week, very early in the morning, the women took the spices they had prepared and went to the tomb. They found the stone rolled away from the tomb, but when they entered, they did not find the body of the Lord Jesus. While they were wondering about this, suddenly two men in clothes that gleamed like lightning stood beside them. In their fright the women bowed down with their faces to the ground, but the men said to them, "Why do you look for the living among the dead? He is not here; he has risen! Remember how he told you, while he was still with you in Galilee: 'The Son of Man must be delivered over to the hands of sinners, be crucified and on the third day be raised again.'" Then they remembered his words.

When they came back from the tomb, they told all these things to the Eleven and to all the others. It was Mary Magdalene, Joanna, Mary the mother of James, and the others with them who told this to the apostles. But they did not believe the women, because their words seemed to them like nonsense. Peter, however, got up and ran to the tomb. Bending over, he saw the strips of linen lying by themselves, and he went away, wondering to himself what had happened.

he very first Easter wasn't all about chocolate and bunny rabbits. Try to imagine the chariot-race roller coaster of emotion these people must have been going through.

Remember Martha just before the resurrection of her brother Lazarus? She believed Jesus when he said she would see Lazarus again . . . just not this week or on this planet (John 11:24). I think it's likely at least some of Jesus' followers still had faith they would see him again—in paradise. Then all kinds of weird stuff happens. It wasn't just that their expectations were shattered; it's more like their expectations were shattered, then stomped on, then picked up, turned inside out, painted magenta and folded into party hats.

I'm not totally satisfied with the usual line we get about the disciples falling apart—hiding like cowards over the Easter weekend. They seemed to have had lots of possible bolt-holes outside the city, but we find them still in Jerusalem, the stronghold of the Sanhedrin and, to some extent, Romans. Wouldn't cowards have fled the city? Even Peter's actions the night of the arrest imply a hint of bravery, following the guards into the very courtyard of the high priest. Did he mean to deny Jesus, or did he mean to be an undercover agent? But I have no trouble agreeing it's the women who were the most transparently faithful. When we pick up their story, they're on their way to the tomb.

On their way to do what at the tomb? Look what they were bringing. Even *they* hadn't spent Saturday night baking cookies for his welcome back party. Their hopes were in the resurrection of the dead, but their money was on funeral wreaths. They'd been buying and mixing spices to bring. These women had no doubt it was a corpse they were on their way to visit.

They're grief-stricken. Perhaps that's why it doesn't appear to have been an exceptionally well-thought-out excursion. It's only when they're almost there, Mark tells us, that they remember the huge boulder blocking the actual tomb (Mark 16:3). Uh-oh, who's going to roll that puppy away? Is this where grief gives way to the feeling of helpless frustration? Nothing's going right . . . we spent all this time preparing these spices and now we won't even be able to mourn him properly! We'll have to leave the spices in front of the stone, outside the tomb.

And, unbelievably, it gets even more discouraging. Can you imagine their feelings when they get to the place? Now helplessness gives way to angry hopelessness: why can't they just leave him alone! They've killed him; isn't that enough? Now they've rolled away the stone, desecrated his tomb and moved his body—before we've even had a chance to say goodbye! Why, why, why?

This is where, just when it seems it can't get any worse, it gets bizarre. There are strangers in space suits at the tomb who act like they know more of the story than they possibly could. How? What? Who are these guys? It's probably only later anyone figures out they must have been angels. Mark and Luke call them men, whereas Matthew and John call them angels. Mark also tells us the women were, quite understandably, terrified. Although Mark says the women told no one, the way it's written in Greek makes it likely that, as they were bidden, they told the disciples but no one else. In much the same way that, earlier, Jesus told one of his healees to show the High Priest what had happened, yet tell no one (Luke 5:14). Matthew sometimes clarifies Mark's ambiguities, and here he confirms that the women went off to tell the disciples, and also that they were filled with a variety of emotions: "afraid yet filled with joy" (Matt. 28:8).

Only John's gospel contains the peculiar story of how the distraught Mary Magdalene hung around a little. She saw another man, who wasn't, apparently, dressed in silver gift wrap like the other guys/angels. She doesn't recognize it's Jesus, and he doesn't let on right away. "Why are you crying? Who is it you are looking for?" he asks (John 20:15). She makes this amnesty offer: "If you have carried him away, tell me . . . and I will get him" (v. 15). No questions asked, she might have added. You've got to love this: she's so right even while she's completely wrong. This is the guy who carried Jesus off! She has caught the culprit—in the very act! After he calls her name and she recognizes him, she goes off and also tells the disciples.

The women's story sounded like nonsense when they tried to explain it to the guys. "Slow down! Shining what? Never mind their clothes—who were they?! Honestly—women!" About the only parts that did get through were that the body was missing and the women were sure Jesus was alive.

But these are Jewish men. In their culture, women were specifically excluded from being considered trustworthy witnesses. What's more, they were clearly confused and agitated. Are they in some sort of state of shock or what? But it wouldn't have been easy for any of the disciples to have kept a level head at that moment either. Worst-case scenario: body's been stolen in order to humiliate Jesus even more. Did they dare to hope for the best-case scenario? On the testimony of women?

It's fitting, though. They're the ones who had been to Golgotha and seen Jesus crucified. If gender issues were left aside, they would be the first and best witnesses to the resurrection.

Peter and one of the other disciples are at least moved to check it out. They run to check it out—John 20:8–9 goes further than Luke 24:12. Seeing might be believing, but it stops way short of understanding. The first stage of the Easter story is not the joy of being reunited with the Lord but the mystery of the empty tomb.

I've sometimes wondered why Christians make such a big deal over the celebration of Christmas, especially compared with Good Friday or Easter. It's true the magi provide a good precedent for the giving of valuable gifts. When they put me in charge of redesigning our culture, I'm going to design a holiday for which all the gifts are bought at great price on Good Friday and then appear on Easter morning, but mysteriously (perhaps even misleadingly) wrapped so everyone wonders, "What is that? What's going on?" That's where the first Easter Sunday began.

Suggestions for Further Thought

In celebrating Easter, are we right to fast-track to certainty about the resurrection as soon as it's sunrise? What might be the point of the uncertainty and mystery in the text?

Good Friday + Easter or Christmas? Which should be more important?

#

He asked them, "Do you have anything here to eat?"

Luke 24:35–44

Then the two told what had happened on the way, and how Jesus was recognized by them when he broke the bread.

While they were still talking about this, Jesus himself stood among them and said to them, "Peace be with you."

They were startled and frightened, thinking they saw a ghost. He said to them, "Why are you troubled, and why do doubts rise in your minds? Look at my hands and my feet. It is I myself! Touch me and see; a ghost does not have flesh and bones, as you see I have."

When he had said this, he showed them his hands and feet. And while they still did not believe it because of joy and amazement, he asked them, "Do you have anything here to eat?" They gave him a piece of broiled fish, and he took it and ate it in their presence.

He said to them, "This is what I told you while I was still with you: Everything must be fulfilled that is written about me in the Law of Moses, the Prophets and the Psalms."

esus was back on earth for forty days. For those with the disposition for writing gospels, there appear to have been no shortage of appearances to choose from. Luke even shows he knows about episodes that he doesn't take the time to recount. The disciples say in Luke 24:34 the Lord had appeared to Simon

Peter, but there's no such story in Luke's gospel. He's selected the ones he includes from a larger number of stories he knows about.

John's choices are pretty cool, but for my money, Luke has the best taste in resurrection stories. I love the Emmaus story and have written about it in my previous book (most excellent Theophiloi). Here's the skinny on it, just to remind you. One late afternoon, two of the disciples are walking home from Jerusalem. On their way they're discussing Jesus' death and trying to make sense of the whole thing. Suddenly they bump into this guy. They don't recognize him, but you and I know it is Jesus. As in the Mary Magdalene story we mentioned last time, he refrains from enlightening them. Instead, he probes them about what they think. Then he explains from Scripture how Messiah had to go through all that stuff. These two prize chumps still don't recognize him, but they take a liking to him. So when they reach their quarters, they invite him in to share their late afternoon meal. Jesus, still in disguise, allows himself to be persuaded. As if he had any intention of going anywhere else . . .

Once inside, he takes up the role of the host at the meal rather than guest. Just as he did at the feeding of the 5,000 and at the Last Supper, Jesus takes the bread, blesses it, breaks it and gives it to them (Luke 24:30). At this point their eyes are opened: it's no stranger; it's Jesus! But he disappears at that moment, without actually getting anything to eat.

Imagine how spooked those two disciples must have been! Did we imagine the whole thing? Did we just imagine that stranger looked like Jesus at the end? But no, someone was here, and whoever it was disappeared. And there's this rubber nose and fake moustache still warm on the table! "They got up and returned at once to Jerusalem" (Luke 24:33). I'll bet they did—with a mixture of terror at the supernatural event they'd witnessed and joy at the thought it might all be true.

The story I had you read is the very next thing that happens in Luke's gospel. The disciples are buzzing and bursting with curiosity and more. Have some of their friends really seen Jesus as they claim? Reports are coming in too fast and thick to be ignored, but too vague and insubstantial to be sure of anything. In the middle of this, Jesus appears.

Everyone seems to recognize him this time. But they react as they did in the earlier walking on water incident. They find it easier to believe this must be some ghostly manifestation of Jesus' life force rather than Jesus physically risen from the dead. So he reassures them in a very physical way. He invites them to touch him and see—and when they do, they find nonghostly flesh and bones.

My favorite bit is what comes in verse 41. They're all standing around open-mouthed, stunned and amazed at the earth-shattering supernatural but flesh-and-bones thing that has evidently just happened. Jesus bursts that little bubble with "So, uh . . . got anything to eat or what?" Well, it's a late supper now; the Emmaus disciples had come all the way back to Jerusalem, having left after mealtime in Emmaus, seven miles away. Presumably, the others have eaten by now as well, given the time of day, but they do manage to find some leftover broiled fish.

Have you seen *Pirates of the Caribbean*? If so, you can imagine what would have happened if Jesus was some kind of undead manifestation instead of back in a complete functioning body: food and drink all over the carpet. Thus, demonstrating his ability to swallow tidily was partially meant to be another answer to the disciples' idea he must be a ghost.

The early church also needed just such an affirmation of the bodily nature of the resurrection—there quickly sprang up heresies like Gnosticism, which argued that bodies and matter were evil and only the non-physical soul was immortal and good. Tartar sauce or not, *their* resurrected Jesus would have had nothing to do with broiled fish.

The importance of Jesus' physicality to the church a hundred years later has made some skeptics suspicious. Having decided ahead of time it is impossible for anyone to really rise from the dead—after all, such things just don't happen—some folks have advanced the theory that perhaps the gospels were written a hundred years later and their authors made up stories to suit this later situation. Faced with heretics who claimed the resurrection wasn't physical, the official church manufactured stories of Jesus polishing off a plate of breaded halibut. It's a nice try, but a few moments of reading the text should put this little idea to rest. If Luke were making up his resurrection stories in order to solve this problem, he would have had his Jesus eat something in the Emmaus story rather than rudely disappearing just after getting to the dinner table!

Instead, we have stories bizarre enough that no devoted Christian would be likely to make them up: a Jesus who pretends to be someone else—a Jesus who rises from the dead, walks into the house and asks, "What's in the fridge?"

He's back!

Suggestions for Further Thought

Jesus has already demonstrated his mastery over death, in the raising of Lazarus, for instance. What's different about this?

Jesus' resurrection body has some pretty unusual properties. The guess is that our resurrection bodies will be like it (1 Cor. 15; 2 Cor. 4:14–5:5). It's all kind of speculative, of course, but fun, to wonder what we'll be like: we've already said that his new body is sometimes difficult to recognize, it seems to be able to walk through walls on occasion, yet it is able to eat. What other properties or abilities does it appear to have?

Preparing for Takeoff

While he was blessing them, he left them and was taken up into heaven.

Luke 24:44–53

He said to them, "This is what I told you while I was still with you: Everything must be fulfilled that is written about me in the Law of Moses, the Prophets and the Psalms."

Then he opened their minds so they could understand the Scriptures. He told them, "This is what is written: The Messiah will suffer and rise from the dead on the third day, and repentance for the forgiveness of sins will be preached in his name to all nations, beginning at Jerusalem. You are witnesses of these things. I am going to send you what my Father has promised; but stay in the city until you have been clothed with power from on high."

When he had led them out to the vicinity of Bethany, he lifted up his hands and blessed them. While he was blessing them, he left them and was taken up into heaven. Then they worshiped him and returned to Jerusalem with great joy. And they stayed continually at the temple, praising God.

know heaven isn't up from here, as if the folks in the space station are any closer to it geographically. You'll read in some commentaries that the phrase "taken up into heaven" is nondirectional—that it's like the English usage of "to take up sewing". Some people think Jesus' so-called ascension in this passage and Acts 1:9 wasn't a trip up into the stratosphere but rather his being enveloped by a foggy cloud and imploding into another dimension like Mr. Mxyzptlk—whoompf. I can't buy that. Acts 1:10 doesn't make any sense if, whatever the location, he didn't at least appear to be going in an upward direction: "They were looking intently up into the sky as he was going." So up isn't the whole story, but it's apparently part of the story.

If you're like me, for a whole day before you fly, your life is dominated by making preparations for the flight. There's all this packing to be done and sorting into carry-on and luggage. You have to chew and stew over what bits of work and reading you'll want to have securely stowed under the seat in front while your eyes are glued to some of the lamentable selections of films.

What preparations Jesus made for his own benefit in advance of his flight aren't obvious. But he does work at preparing the disciples for departure time. They'd have liked it if he'd done a bit more—they would have peppered him with questions if they'd had any inkling they were going to be more or less on their own for the next few thousand years. Typical Jesus, though, giving you enough to work out the details yourself.

There are at least three points to his preparation program. First, he helps them get the story straight. He carefully grounds them in the basics in those forty days, explaining to them in Luke 24:45 how all the Scriptures pointed to and confirm the events that have happened in their lifetime, the center of time.

Second, he gets them in gear to become witnesses of what had happened. Luke doesn't talk so much about this in his gospel but emphasizes it when he covers the same ground in his second volume, Acts. There Jesus tells them, "You will be my witnesses in Jerusalem, and in all Judea and Samaria, and to the ends of the earth" (Acts 1:8). The message will spread out in widening ripples. Significantly, it will spread in ripples that continue beyond the edges of the little pond of Judaism.

It's Matthew's version, though, that is the most well known. The inclusion of non-Jews is almost taken for granted as the command focuses on the task rather than the sphere of operations: "Go and make disciples of all nations, baptizing them in the name of the Father and of the Son and of the Holy Spirit, and teaching them to obey everything I have commanded you" (Matt. 28:19–20, often called "the Great Commission").

Third, Jesus prepares his followers for the "gift" they're going to receive after he leaves: the gift of the Holy Spirit. This is a bigger deal for them than it might seem to you. In the Old Testament world, the Holy Spirit was a special occasion sort of thing. People would be given the Holy Spirit for certain particular tasks. In the old days, he was just visiting. Jesus is talking about an era where the Holy Spirit moves in.

Not many people talk about it much, but I'll guess most non-charismatic Christians, if we can be honest with ourselves here for a few minutes, have trouble feeling very excited about this gift. Like socks on Christmas morning, we're grateful and all, yeah. But we could get on pretty well with the socks we've already got or could buy our own.

I promise you, you don't want me to answer this with details of what the Holy Spirit does for a living. You can find plenty of books and experts on that subject, giving conflicting messages, just the same way you can find plenty of books and experts giving you conflicting reasons why being in a stable, loving relationship is good for you. But they all agree the Holy Spirit is a good thing, an indispensably good thing. "Clothed with power from on high," Jesus called it in Luke 24:49.

There's no doubt Peter and the other guys didn't instantly turn into brilliant and morally pure paragons after getting themselves singed by the flames at Pentecost. The Holy Spirit is a gift, but he's not Cinderella's fairy godmother. But on the other hand, they did change—they moved with a new purpose and a new boldness and were being transformed.

So ask yourself this: being in love—really and truly in love—does that make a difference? Does that make you more in touch with yourself and others, does that make you instantly good at being in a relationship—a good listener, a good communicator? Uh, yes and no. Eventually it will, if you stay in love and committed to love. But couldn't you go out and find people who are better listeners and communicators who aren't, in fact, in love? Yeah, maybe. Let me ask you another question: have you honestly never noticed how a pregnant woman, even before it shows, glows? If the beginning of a human being living inside you can make a difference, is it so strange to think God living inside you might also make a real difference, however unable we are to measure it with a ruler, light meter or IQ test? It's like being in love. Or rather, since God is love—it's like Love being in you.

After Jesus has prepared the disciples in these three ways, then, the elevator bell dings and it's cloud city. Then they do something amazing for Jews to do: they worship him (24:52). Some people will tell you that they didn't, that Luke has made the assumptions of the later Christian church in his description of these Jews. Oh, really? Explain the next sentence, then! They didn't go to a church after that; they didn't even go back to their homes. They returned to Jerusalem, and like the Jews Luke knows they still are, "they stayed continually at the temple, praising God" (24:53). No Christian, writing from the perspective of the second century church, would close his first volume with those important Christians praising God in the doomed Jewish temple!

Luke starts the book of Acts by saying his gospel was about what Jesus began to do, as if Acts is about what he continues to do, even if he does so through the apostles. Thanks to the way Jesus prepared his disciples for his take off, what happens in Acts is nearly as amazing as what happened in the gospel.

But that'll have to wait for another book.

Suggestions for Further Thought

On the one hand, some traditions, like my own, tend to ignore the Holy Spirit and let him get on with whatever he does. On the other hand, I've been to other churches where they'll take a passage like John 3 and spend the whole 45 minutes of the sermon on the Holy Spirit, although the passage implies that the Spirit's work is mysterious (v. 8) while explaining the actions and motives of the Son and Father (vv. 13–21). Which tradition are you in? How do you reckon you can learn from the other?

In a sense, the entire Bible is about what God began to do in this world he's made and watched over. He continues his work through us, his people. Have you ever observed it—known someone who was where they should be, doing what they should be doing? Have you ever felt it yourself? What would it take to be in that zone right now? Is it worth it?

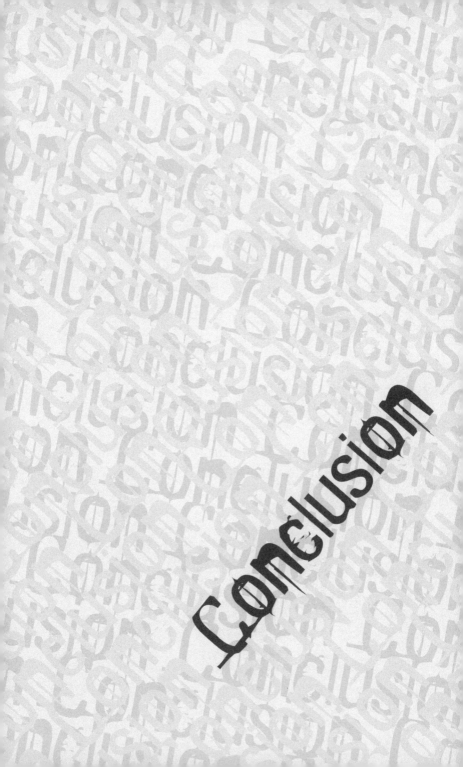

Conclusion

The Imitation of Christ ... or Not?

Christ suffered for you, leaving you an example.

1 Peter 2:19-24

For it is commendable if you bear up under the pain of unjust suffering because you are conscious of God. But how is it to your credit if you receive a beating for doing wrong and endure it? But if you suffer for doing good and you endure it, this is commendable before God. To this you were called, because Christ suffered for you, leaving you an example, that you should follow in his steps.

"He committed no sin,
and no deceit was found in his mouth."

When they hurled their insults at him, he did not retaliate; when he suffered, he made no threats. Instead, he entrusted himself to him who judges justly. "He himself bore our sins" in his body on the cross, so that we might die to sins and live for righteousness; "by his wounds you have been healed."

s imitating Jesus? Shouldn't it be the other way around? When I was growing up, I was taught that Jesus is fully human and fully divine. But the way I imagined it was much more like God doing an imitation of a human being. This seemed to have two main payoffs. One, he spent Christmas as a cute little baby; and two, he wasn't like the character we referred to as the Holy Ghost. Jesus was solid and walked around on the planet and could talk to people without the use of hovering doves or tongues of flame. He looked and acted like us, but he was the second person of the Trinity just under his street clothes.

For much of my Christian life, Jesus' unique divine nature simply eclipsed his ordinary and mundane human nature. It only seems sensible that the divine is going to eclipse the merely human. And in our culture that denies Christ's deity (or anyone else's for that matter), the emphasis is perhaps healthier than it sounds. He was a different kind of being than we are, and his whole reason for coming was to do things that we could not do and would be inappropriate for us to try to do, being neither perfect nor God.

I had no trouble with the many verses in Scripture that talk about our becoming perfect and becoming like him, our being transformed into his likeness (2 Cor. 3:18; 1 John 3:2). When the trumpet blows and he comes hanging ten off his surfboard of clouds, all sorts of things about us are going to change: new versions of our bodies and upgraded minds and wills (Phil. 3:21; 1 Cor. 13:12). But all that is God making us like Christ in paradise, a different matter than our doing it ourselves on a Tuesday morning.

But trying to imitate Jesus is a suspicious concept, like trying to earn God's love by acting just right. Jesus fulfilled the law for us, in our place, precisely because we are unable to do so. To work at trying to be like him in that is to miss the point. He died that we might live. We were sinners; he was perfect. He took our sins upon himself—the work on the cross that only he could accomplish. Imitate him? The whole point is that we're diametrically opposed!

But unlikely as it seems, this is what the New Testament tells us to do. And not just on Tuesdays. "Those who would be my disciples must deny themselves and take up their cross daily and follow me", and "Those who do not carry their cross and follow me cannot be my disciples" (Luke 9:23; 14:27). Paul told his troublesome Corinthians, "Imitate me, just as I also imitate Christ" (1 Cor. 11:1 NKJV). Apparently the church's leaders are to function as models of Christ for their people in verses like 2 Thessalonians 3:9 and Hebrews 13:7.

So maybe my reaction was a wrong one. Perhaps we really are meant to act the way Jesus acted: to imitate him. Maybe those bumper stickers with "What would Jesus do?" aren't such a bad way of conceiving of Christianity after all. Is the "uniqueness of Christ" a doctrinal smoke screen behind which we hide so we don't have to live his life of self-sacrifice? Did he deliberately become human, setting his divinity aside, so our aim could be to copy the way he lived?

That's going too far. We are becoming more like Christ, but in the process, we are becoming more like what we ourselves were meant to be. God does not want thousands of clones of Jesus. There are things we're meant to do despite the fact that Jesus never did them, and things that Jesus did that we're not called to try to duplicate.

The cross is the prime example, despite "Take up your cross and follow me". Jesus spoke in parables and symbols; the authors of the epistles write more plainly. None of them call the reader to "take up your cross". Carry your own load: yes. Bear suffering as Christ did: yes. Look for a cross to die on for others: no way.

Paul, who you'll remember imitated Christ to the Corinthians, still reacts with horror when some cry, "I follow Paul." He writes, "Was Paul crucified for you? Were you baptized into the name of Paul?" (1 Cor. 1:12–13). Imitating Christ does not mean becoming another Christ.

Jesus had a role in salvation that Christians can never fill and should never try to. Although the 1 Peter 2 passage calls us to be like Jesus in suffering (vv. 20–21), it goes on to make crystal clear Jesus' uniqueness in suffering for us in verse 24: "'He himself bore our sins' in his body on the tree, so that we might die to sins and live for righteousness; 'by his wounds you have been healed.'" There are many passages about our suffering, but crucifixion is not something most of us are to go through, except symbolically, to put to death our sinfulness (Gal. 5:24). Over and over, we're told by different New Testament authors that Jesus' death was a "once for all" thing (Rom. 6:10; Heb. 7:27; 1 Peter 3:18).

In this book we've looked at four main facets of Jesus' life. The same principle of imitation holds in all of them. We are to imitate him in teaching and spreading the word, but not necessarily to memorize and duplicate his teaching. The content of the teaching of the earliest church as recorded in the book of Acts bears little resemblance to the content of Jesus' own, even when a close disciple like Peter is doing the talking. He knew that Jesus always spoke in parables, yet Peter never does. He knew that Jesus spoke cryptically of himself and made the kingdom of God central. The apostles' teaching, by contrast, speaks plainly and focuses on Jesus himself. We are to be like him in some ways but not in others.

So also with the miracles and healings. Again, the earliest church did some of this, but to nothing like the extent of Jesus' ministry. We saw that although Jesus said his followers would do greater things than he had done, it may or may not mean what we regard as supernatural. Not even the most fervent believer in "What would Jesus do?" feels called to gather 5,000 people in one place in order to multiply some white bread and tuna. Our imitation of Christ is probably not meant to include making up travel time by shortcuts on foot over water or commanding storms to cease. But we must be open to astonishing things coming from God and the miraculous happening through us, even things that Jesus never did.

In Jesus' spirituality and radical behaviour, we have a tension between the way he not only allows but encourages the Twelve to call God "*Abba*, Father" on the one hand and the way he presumes to be doing the Father's work on the other. Not many will be called to imitate Christ in the way he argued with the most religious and most educated people of his day; not many will be called to imitate him in overturning money tables. Nor do I recommend implying, as he did, a more intimate relationship with the Father than anyone else.

And as we've been arguing, despite our identification with him in the cross and resurrection, we are not necessarily to imitate him in seeking a cross, nor to imitate his Gethsemane conviction that his death was the only way forward.

Overall, it seems that we are more likely to be called to imitate his attitudes than his specific actions. But those attitudes must be acted upon—lived out. Thomas à Kempis's amazing book *The Imitation of Christ* recommends just this. We are to have the same mind as Christ in his willingness to be a servant and set himself to one side. We are, like him, to focus on the needs of others. We are to imitate his unswerving dedication and commitment to God, wherever that might take us. But we stay ourselves; or, rather, by being conformed to him we become ourselves, distinct from each other and him despite the family resemblance. Through the Spirit, we begin taking on his ways of relating to God and other people and self.

So "What would Jesus do?" only works in a limited way. Someday you may find yourself in a situation in which you are called to play the saxophone. What would Jesus do? We have no record of him doing that. But God may want *you* to. When you do, though, play it in the way that Jesus would have done it. Say, "This is for you", rather than, "Am I not cool?" In a way it's not you who plays but Christ who plays through you. So we do things that Jesus never did, but we do them Jesus-style.

Suggestions for Further Thought

Is it contradictory to think God loves us just as we are and yet expects us to change?

Is "What would Jesus do?" a good maxim to live by?

Back to Earth in Time for Supper

**I stand at the door and knock.
If anyone hears my voice
and opens the door,
I will come in and eat with them,
and they with me.**

Revelation 3:14-22

"To the angel of the church in Laodicea write: These are the words of the Amen, the faithful and true witness, the ruler of God's creation. I know your deeds, that you are neither cold nor hot. I wish you were either one or the other! So, because you are lukewarm—neither hot nor cold—I am about to spit you out of my mouth. You say, 'I am rich; I have acquired wealth and do not need a thing.' But you do not realize that you are wretched, pitiful, poor, blind and naked. I counsel you to buy from me gold refined in the fire, so you can become rich; and white clothes to wear, so you can cover your shameful nakedness; and salve to put on your eyes, so you can see.

Those whom I love I rebuke and discipline. So be earnest, and repent. Here I am! I stand at the door and knock. If anyone hears my voice and opens the door, I will come in and eat with them, and they with me.

To those who are victorious, I will give the right to sit with me on my throne, just as I was victorious and sat down with my Father on his throne. Whoever has ears, let them hear what the Spirit says to the churches."

ohn the Baptist ate bugs (Mark 1:6). In contrast to him, Jesus struck people as a pretty good eater. Those looking for an excuse to dislike him called him a glutton and a drunkard (Luke 7:33–34). And we've seen that he did seem to have meals with a lot of different people. It wasn't always like that, though. One of my favorite stories in this regard is in Mark 3. In verse 20, Jesus and his disciples are so busy with a crowd that they don't even have time to eat. Now remember I told you Jesus was Jewish? Well, that goes for his mother as well, obviously. And in the next verse, she and the family hear about the incident and head out to see him (Mark 3:21, 31). "Whaddya mean you're too busy for supper? You're nothing but skin and bones. Eat something already. For me. And would it kill you to phone me once in a while?" His disciples do the same thing to him in John 4:31: "Rabbi, eat something." And in the next verse he replies, "I have food . . . you know nothing about." His mealtime habits center on God's will and people rather than food.

This passage about Jesus knocking at the door and waiting for a reply is often used for evangelism. It's a powerful picture, appropriate for all sorts of uses. But the author of Revelation has fence-sitting Christians in mind rather than God-hating atheists. It is those who are lukewarm the Lord will spit out of his mouth. There may be a whole lot of spitting going on with today's church as well as with the church of the Laodiceans.

I've often thought about Jesus knocking on the door. It's funny, though, until I started writing this book, I never paid too much attention to what happens when and if you open that door. Jesus comes in and has supper with you and you with him. And now, of course, these words remind me of two resurrection appearances we've already looked at. But in neither passage does Jesus knock and wait. On the Emmaus road, he does the opposite of asking to come in; he pretends (Luke 24:28) that he's going farther and the two believers have to talk him into coming in to share a meal. The other incident is the one in which he just showed up and asked about food. No knocking there; there wasn't even a door mentioned. It might have been one of those times that he just came in through the walls (Luke 24:36).

But now, he knocks. And he wants to come in and share this table fellowship of acceptance we've talked about. Him with you and you with him. And your dining room table isn't the only place he wants to sit with you. Revelation goes on to say that those who are his will sit with him on his throne. I don't think Revelation means for us to take this completely literally, or else we're talking about either a huge bench of a throne or a long wait for a turn. Like the image of Jesus standing at the door knocking, this is picture language, of which the book of Revelation has a lot.

The first readers, though, would have been struck by the contrast between the Jesus who has a throne given to him by God and the way that he stands and knocks meekly at the door, waiting and hoping for our attention. But this is so like him, so much a picture of the incarnation. He's the king who doesn't intend to commandeer; the king who's willing to share his throne if we'll share our spaghetti. How can you say no?

We've come a long way together in this book—looked at a lot of stories covering some of the variety of passages about Jesus in the New Testament. But now at the book of Revelation, we've come full circle. The first story we looked at involved Jesus inviting Peter and the boys to bring some of *their* fish.

And so it still is. Yeah, okay, I've made more out of the mealtime motif than strictly necessary. But that self-giving, sharing and table fellowship is still on his mind today. You know he's knocking. And if you've got a little bit you're willing to share with him, he'll be there. And he brings more to the table than you do. He's like that. He has always wanted to be at your service.

He still visits earth for supper. Or lunch. Or breakfast. Or brunch. Or afternoon tea. Or. . .

Suggestions for Further Thought

Rereading this to write these thought questions, it occurs to me that I may be over-playing the meekness of Jesus at the door. It's in the context of rebuking and disciplining (Rev. 3:19). He is standing at the door, but he's not just knocking quietly in verse 20, because it goes on to say, "If anyone hears my voice and opens . . .". So he's yelling too! Are there times when yelling and banging have been your experience of Jesus?

There's a sense in which saying, "Come in, Jesus", is something we do once at conversion, and the Holy Spirit comes in and changes us forever. There's another sense in which saying, "Come in, Jesus", is something we need to say constantly and consistently, which may be truer to Revelation 3. How do you resolve the tension between those two?

Scripture Index

Bold type is used when the Scripture passage indicated is the main text for the encounter.

No attempt has been made to list parallel passages in gospels (unless the book specifically mentions them).

Subject Index

Note to the reader: In a book with such short "chapters" you may find the Table of Contents a help in finding topics as well.

Bold type is used to indicate subjects that have an alphabetic proximity and curious conceptual affinity.

Jesus Asked.
What He Wanted to Know

Conrad Gempf

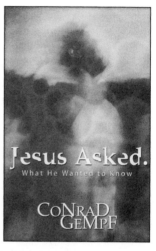

In the Gospels, when people asked Jesus a question, he often replied with one of his own: "Good teacher, what must I do to inherit eternal life?" "Why do you call me good?" British author Conrad Gempf invites readers to look at these questions and discover Jesus' motivation. What could the second person of the Trinity want to know that he doesn't already? Gempf concludes that Jesus wants to know where we stand. He doesn't need to know more facts; he wants to know us.

Softcover: 0-310-24773-X

Pick up a copy today at your favorite bookstore!

ZONDERVAN™

GRAND RAPIDS, MICHIGAN 49530 USA

WWW.ZONDERVAN.COM